Once A Marine...

Honoring the Life of My Father
Captain Roger Jamieson, USMCR (Ret.)

To LeRoy & Ginger,

Thank you for your
service & my freedom!

JAY A. JAMIESON, M.D.

Grateful acknowledgement is made to the following for permission to reprint copyrighted material.

George Feifer, selections from "Tennozan: The Battle for Okinawa and the Atomic Bomb" Ticknor and Fields, Copyright 1992

Hal Leonard Corporation for use of excerpts of lyrics from "Leader of the Band", Dan Fogleberg, Copyright 1981

Mainstage Management/Jericho Beach Music for use of excerpts of lyrics from "Begin," Nicky Mehta, Copyright 2006

Paramount Pictures Corporation, an excerpt from "Flags of Our Fathers"/ courtesy of DreamWorks Pictures, Copyright 2006

Random House Publishing, for selections from An "Album of Memories" and "The Greatest Generation" Copyrights 2001 and 1998, respectively, Tom Brokaw

Mike Shatzkin, selections from "The Ballplayers", William Morrow and Company, Copyright 1990

Sports Publishing, L.L.C, selections from "The Cleveland Indians Encyclopedia," 3rd Edition, by Russell Schneider, Copyright 2004

Stars and Stripes, photographs by Donovan Brooks, 1995

Universal Studios, excerpts from "Cloak & Dagger," Tom Holland, Copyright 1984

First published by Dog Ear Publishing
4010 W. 86th Street, Ste H
Indianapolis, IN 46268
www.dogearpublishing.net

ISBN: 978-159858-829-3

This book is printed on acid-free paper.

Printed in the United States of America

This book is dedicated to:

The Sixth Marine Division

2nd Squad, 3rd Platoon, C-1-25, 4th Marine Division
Especially David Dougherty, Jack Jones and James "Sammy" Sampson

Rowan Elliott and Finley Rose Jamieson, who represent the next generation.
May the lessons learned live on.

Table of Contents

Foreword and Acknowledgements

"Once a Marine—always a Marine." I heard that expression countless times growing up in reference to my father, Roger Jamieson. As kids growing up in the fifties we learned that to be a U.S. Marine was something special and unique. And although we noticed their cockiness could be a bit abrasive to others, we also noted that there was a respect and awe given them. Later in my life, I would meet a Sixth Marine Division veteran in Okinawa, Charles Seltzer, who summed it all up, as a Marine Corps Band came marching by in review, "It's hard to be humble when you're the best."

My father was a World War II era Marine officer. He raised his four children using many of the lessons in leadership he learned from 1942 to 1946. He was not, thankfully, 'The Great Santini' prototype. He was more or less what NCOs would characterize as a gentleman officer, which meant along with his toughness and disciplined life there was plenty of justice, mercy, heart and humor to go around.

He was one of 17,000,000 Americans who volunteered to put their lives on hold and their lives on the line to protect our nation from evil fascist states that threatened our shores. While each person's story is unique, he would say that he didn't do anything special or different from anyone else at that time. In the end he, his extended family and neighborhood sacrificed and suffered like all Americans did during the war: separation, loneliness, illness, injury, death of friends and loved ones.

Tom Brokaw has written down several stories of World War II veterans in his now famous book, <u>The Greatest Generation</u>. As Mr. Brokaw so eloquently wrote, "They fought great odds and a late start, but they did not protest. At a time in their lives when their days and nights should have been filled with innocent adventure, love and the lessons of the workaday world, they were fighting, often hand to hand in the most primitive conditions possible…." Well, Tom, I know you had 17,000,000 to choose from, but you missed a good one here.

But while my father would say he did nothing extraordinary, my point is my father did volunteer; he did not back down from his duty. He faced his fears and he faced the enemy. He contributed to the war effort. During his four years of active duty as a U.S. Marine, he traveled over 32,000 miles, mostly by ship (which might explain his reluctance to go on cruises later in life) but also by train, plane, jeep and foot. He remembered the date of departure and the name of every ship he was on. He remembered the locations of every assignment location and many of the names of his fellow Marines.

He suffered from fleas and jungle rot, Dengue Fever, dysentery and Hepatitis A. He was wounded twice; he suffered from the loss of his entire platoon and his beloved cousin. The latter two experiences he silently mourned and carried with him his entire life.

This book had its origin many years ago, but the process for me began in 1994 as you will see. I did not begin to organize and write down my thoughts and experiences until August 2007, just after the death of my father. I knew my dad, the ever self-effacing type, would not have stood for such attention. One of the many nicknames my dad gave me was "Last Word Louie"; so it will not be too surprising to my family that I would get in the last word. In the end, this is my attempt to honor the life of my beloved father. I have been one lucky boy to have a dad like this. This is my way of saying thanks to a wonderful dad.

The work on this book has been a form of therapy for me. It has allowed me to creatively mourn the loss of my number one hero; the man who had the most positive influence in my life. Many times while talking with my dad and interviewing his acquaintances, reading countless accounts of the war or watching documentaries, I would fantasize about being there. "What would it have been like? I wish I could have seen my dad, young, healthy and strong; to have been a casual observer there." I realize that is not possible, but thanks to the stories told by him and his friends, I have been granted a peek and thus attempted to recreate the past. Many of the stories I pass on I had heard before, but several were new to me.

I hope the stories told will be of comfort and a similar therapeutic benefit to my mother, brothers and sister and to our entire extended family and friends. We all miss Dad, our platoon leader. We miss him every day.

This story is also about a cousin I never got to meet: David Leslie Dougherty. War's hell denied our family a relationship with him and what would have been his family. The journey that started out to help heal the war wounds of my dad inevitably had to lead to and through his Cousin David's story and miraculously to his surviving squad.

And I also wrote these experiences so that my children and nephews and nieces could have added insight and reinforce what they already know: their grandfather as an honorable and brave man— a man of impeccable integrity... someone in whom they could be proud. I hope this book will be a reference point for their children to learn.

One feature of this book is that it is supplemented by a web site: www.onceamarinebook.info, which contains a more extensive photo gallery, more information about Charlie Jamieson's professional baseball career, links to some video footage, and e-mail for comments. It is my hope that this feature will enhance your reading experience.

But I could not have done this work alone. I would like to thank several people who contributed to the effort: Sharon Helton, my office manager, who quietly prayed for me daily during this process. To God be the Glory! Thank you Robyn Scott, my office I.T. expert, who assisted me with the manuscript printing and storage. Thanks also to Jane Taliaferro, my transcriptionist, who not only did an outstanding job typing the first draft, but by being the first person to read the rough draft encouraged me with positive feedback about the storyline.

Over these fourteen years since 1994, I have written and talked with many of the Greatest Generation. What an honor that has been. Thanks to Sgt. Jack Grant, Leo Kelly, William Hewitt, Charlie Wolf, Edgar J. "Lance" La Lancette and all the members of 2nd Squad, 3rd Platoon, C-1-25, 4th Marine Division for allowing me to share your story with others. Also thanks go to John Stone of the 4th Marine Division Association, Rex Dillow, Bill Whitaker, and Ed Pesely formerly of the 6th Marine Division.

Thanks to George Feifer for expanding my understanding about the battle of Okinawa through his book, Tennozan, and Michelle Wist for helping me locate Rex Dillow. Thank you Shizuo Uizumi. Thanks to Bruce Brown for advising me about finding World War II records. Thank you SSgt. Jerry Johnson for the way you have honored my dad.

Thanks to Myrene Garbaccio Pfaff and Don Hall for stories from the Paterson days. Thanks also to my sister Lynn and brother Doug and cousin Bill Ganon, for allowing me to print some of their thoughts. And thanks to my brother David for finding a map I had made of Dad's World War II travels. Thank you to my son David who aided me in the world of word processing.

And a special thanks to the "Lost Jamiesons", as I have come to call them. Although I had had little to no contact with this branch of the clan before, they proved to be enthusiastic supporters of the project and added valuable perspective: John Jamieson, son of Charlie Jamieson, Donald Jamieson, son of David Jamieson and Roberta McCarthy, daughter of Sara Jamieson Dechert. These cousins of my dad and David Dougherty took the time to read over the family history section of the book and correct, confirm, clarify and collaborate new information and insights. Thanks again.

Thank you Mrs. Fawcett, my high school college writing teacher who always demanded the highest standard. Thank you, Barbara Castleman of Ladywebpro.com, for creating a top notch web site and Matt Murry and the staff of Dog Ear Publishing of Indianapolis, Indiana for printing my book.

I also want to give a special thank you to Dr. David Elmgren, who personally guided me through my father's 10 month battle with prostate cancer. Your kindness to me will not be forgotten.

My mother, Betty, read, edited and put her stamp of approval on this book. Thank you so much for your assistance and for keeping the project under cover. But most of all, I owe a huge debt of gratitude to my wife, Kelly, who encouraged me to start this project and patiently listened and advised me throughout this process. I never would have been able to do this without your love, help, and encouragement.

Jay A. Jamieson, M.D.

Honor your Father and your Mother, as Yahweh your God has commanded you, so that you may have long life and may prosper in the country which Yahweh your God is giving you.

— Deuteronomy 5:16 New Jerusalem Bible

TWO MEN

Two boys——- more like brothers, played
carefree together in the Spring's warm light.
Two boys——-more like brothers, grew
with separate fates as a World turned dark.

Two young men, obeying the Call
were willing to sacrifice all
For honor, duty and faithfulness
to God, Country and brother.

Two young men left safe havens with mother's prayers
To battle the enemy on far away shores.
Both chose the road less traveled
So that Good could triumph over Evil——-
Knowing that there was no promise of return.

Two young men on separate missions——-
One almost made it to the shore; the ultimate price paid.
No greater love is known than this——-that he would lay down
His life for his brothers.

The other voluntarily faced certain death on a bitter hill,
No turning back, he became a man.
And, by God's omniscient grace was spared
To tell his children's children the lessons learned.
He did what was right and would never have to look back in doubt.

Two men——- more like brothers, separated
For a time by war's hell.
Will someday play together again
Like carefree boys in God's warm light.

No wars.
No tears.
Just Peace.

That is God's eternal promise.

Jay Jamieson, November 1994

Dedicated to PFC David Dougherty, USMC & Capt. Roger Jamieson,
USMC (ret.)

Cousins Roger Jamieson and David Dougherty on leave in Waikiki

BACKGROUND

"It was a common trait of the Greatest Generation not to discuss the difficult times and how those times shaped their lives, but now, in their twilight years, more and more members of that remarkable group… are determined to tell their experiences."

Tom Brokaw, An Album of Memories

CHAPTER 1

D-Day Plus Fifty Years

June in the Willamette Valley, Salem, Oregon, should be a wonderful time of year. The weather is warming up; the constant rains of fall, winter, and spring are finally letting up a bit. The valley is emerald green with trees and grass...yes, grass. The Willamette Valley is the grass-seed capital of the world, and before there is grass seed, there must be grass pollen. The Willamette Valley leads the world in grass pollen counts and if you are a hay-fever sufferer like me, June spells misery while the fescues and ryes pollinate.

I am a family physician - a baby boomer - in a small, three-doctor clinic eight miles north of my home in Salem, Oregon, in the town of Keizer, Oregon. June brings in countless patients with the repeat annoying symptoms of hay fever - runny, itchy eyes and nose. My patients always tell me, "This is the worst year ever." I don't try to dissuade them but they say this every year.

Today was like any other day. I read my Bible in the early morning and scanned the local newspaper. There was an article about the 50th anniversary of the invasion of Normandy. I probably didn't give it much thought. I rushed off to work.

I was raised the son of a U.S. Marine, World War II vintage. My dad traveled in the South and Central Pacific. He always felt that the U.S. Army in Europe got all the publicity, and what the Marines had done was pretty much forgotten, obscure, and eclipsed by General Eisenhower and the European Theater. I believe he was right. Some of that underdog attitude rubbed off on me over the years.

Work that day was the usual: The endless phone messages, prescription refills, countless questions, seeing patients, and running the office.

My drive to and from work usually was my only down time, where I could daydream, listen to the radio, and gear up on the way in, or wind down on the commute home.

Dinner at home was the usual three-ring circus. Prior to having children, I had often fantasized what dinnertime would be like when we did have children. I visualized more of a "Leave it to Beaver" setting with fine dining and well groomed and mannered children listening attentively to the wisdom of their parents. Children would appropriately respond to questions and queries of the day. Siblings would, of course, display mutual admiration while dining. Before dessert perhaps we would all join in some meaningful family devotionals and cap it all off with a rousing harmonious song rivaling the Von Trapp Family Singers. Of course, nothing close ever resembled that idyllic pipe dream. The following example would be typical. We would be sitting around the table; my wife and I are serving up food to three boys and their younger sisters. It is noisy and chaotic; the kind of noise and chaos that ushers in indigestion. While I am reprimanding one son about teasing his sister, my second son, Daniel, is telling his gullible and sensitive younger sister, Erin, that she looks like this and opens his mouth with half chewed pizza. Erin is mortified and says crying, "Oh yeah? Well, you look like this!" and throws a slice of pepperoni right at Dan's head. He ducks and the pizza sticks to my wife's beautiful hutch window directly behind. I now look up to see Erin in tears, Dan with a sheepish look on his face and a slice of pizza slowly sliding down the hutch. I find out what happened and send Dan to his room. Maalox anyone?

My wife, Kelly, and I have five children. On this day in June, 1994, David was 14 at the time and an eighth-grader playing Babe Ruth baseball and recovering from a tibial fracture in his right leg that he suffered in a January skiing accident. Daniel, age 12, was playing major-league baseball for Judson Little League. Joe, age 9, self-proclaimed "the best in baseball," was playing triple-A (a step below majors). Holly, age 6, and Erin, age 3, were constantly being hauled around from one game to the next watching their brothers play.

I was up to my ears in commitment with Judson Little League at that time as a board member and field maintenance supervisor - although this year I had taken a sabbatical from coaching. After coaching for six years I needed to recharge my batteries. On June 6, 1994, through some stroke of luck or more likely divine providence, my kids had no games. I was not on call and the evening was free.

Ask any of my kids, my wife, or my new daughter-in-law, Sara, and they will tell you I am somewhat of a TV junkie. I enjoy news shows, talk shows and historical or biographical documentaries. I don't read fiction. I do enjoy reading books that will give me insight into current events about our world and our culture. But it would not surprise anyone that after dinner and a tedious day at the office, I would find myself upstairs channel-surfing. Since we did not have cable TV (I loathed MTV) surfing the six channels didn't take long. I watched NBC Nightly News that night. Tom Brokaw was on assignment reporting from the beaches of Normandy.

I remember watching with interest as he walked the beaches with the returning veterans. The guys were in their late 60s, early 70s, not as lean and not as mean as they were 50 years earlier. Most were wearing some type of commemorative hat with a logo. Two things captivated me as I watched the segment. First, the absolute reverence that Tom Brokaw displayed when he walked with these men. He treated them with honor and respect as he asked them questions and let them speak. The second thing I noticed was the World War II veterans. Their memories were vivid. They remembered every detail as if the adrenaline of that day 50 years ago had indelibly seared their memory. They were telling stories about D-Day as if it had happened yesterday.

These veterans seemed like ordinary men like my dad. It was not uncommon to see them choke up when any mention came of their fallen brothers. As I watched these veterans on T.V., I could sense their sadness and guilt as they talked about their lost friends. The survivors, to a man, honored and reverenced the fallen as the true heroes — a theme I would hear over and over again over the next 14 years. Something hooked me; something began stirring inside me as I watched Tom Brokaw with those men. I found out later in 1998, when reading his book, The Greatest Generation that the same thing happened to Tom Brokaw in 1984 when he visited Normandy with NBC News for the 40th anniversary. He underwent "a life-changing experience." Tom Brokaw had discovered a goldmine and he inspired all of us to stop and listen to these great men and women who were our parents, like my dad and mom, Roger and Betty Jamieson.

Later that evening I watched a two-hour special on ABC with Peter Jennings, which documented the entire D-Day invasion including the 101st Airborne, the gliders, the armada, and the various landings of the Canadians, the British, and the U.S. troops.

I was captivated by the enormity of the invasion and the absolute guts of these 18 to 20-year-old boys who landed and jumped into combat. Against seemingly hopeless odds, they kept moving forward and broke through the German defenses. Heroic does not begin to describe what happened.

I started thinking about my own dad. My mom, Betty, my sister Lynn, my brothers David and Douglas and I had all heard a few things over the years, but not much. Dad did not talk a lot about his experiences. We had seen a few pictures of him in the South Pacific. We knew he had fought in Okinawa and was wounded fighting on a place called Sugar Loaf Hill. We knew that his cousin, David Leslie Dougherty, was killed in action some-where in the Pacific. We also knew not to pry too much. These memories were sacred ground and Dad did not talk about them.

We knew Dad was proud to be a Marine. We were raised to believe that the Marines were the best of all the services in the U.S. military. Our folks had taken us to Washington, D.C. in the summer of 1961 to view, amongst other things, Quantico, where Dad had trained to be an officer. I distinctly recall he was excited to drive around looking at his old barracks and the seven hills obstacle course. We stood at the U.S. Marine Corps Memorial. We kids were impressed, but I believe my dad was awed and his heart gladdened that the Marines were remembered. We visited Arlington National Cemetery and watched the solemn ceremony, the changing of the guard at the Tomb of the Unknown Soldier. On Friday night we all went to 8th and I, U.S. Marine Corps Headquarters and watched on a sultry evening the silent color guard perform to perfection. That evening forever etched in my mind that the Marines really were the best.

Dad was a proud Marine - once a Marine, always a Marine.

As a kid, I can recall asking him questions about his World War II experiences. Most of what I knew about World War II was from black-and-white movies starring Audie Murphy or John Wayne killing the Germans or the Japanese. It was mostly corny Hollywood renditions of heroics, but we bought all of that hook, line, and sinker as children. The neighborhood boys on Tilley Avenue in suburban northern New Jersey where I grew up, would reenact battles we had seen on T.V. The agreed upon rule in our neighbor-hood for all mock battles was first shot you were wounded and it always took a second shot to die. I believe this was folklore we perpetuated from watching these war movies. And of course the glorious thing to do was to kill the Germans or the Japanese.

I know I asked Dad, when I was a boy, if he killed any Japanese. I remember he recoiled by my question and quietly said, "I suppose I did, Jay." The answer was ambiguous and I remember his response sent me a polite but firm message that I had crossed over the line. His body language and tone told me that there was nothing bravado or heroic about killing another human being.

Now I was 40 years old, sitting there watching the 50th anniversary of D-Day Europe and wondering about my dad. He was almost 74 years old. I wondered if there would be any recognition of the Battle for Okinawa which occurred April 1 through June 21, 1945. The 50th anniversary would be next year. Did anybody remember the Pacific Theater? I didn't know. Dad's only contact with the Marine Corps was that he was a member of the Marine Corps Memorial Club, a hotel in San Francisco. He had a plaque made to commemorate his cousin, David, and had it mounted at the hotel. Dad did not belong to veterans' organizations. He wasn't a joiner. He was more or less a loner. He was quite sociable with his small circle of friends, but he stayed away from "reliving the glory days of World War II." Dad was out of the loop when it came to World War II, Marines, reunions, and the like.

After three hours of couch potato TV viewing, I had been smitten. Something deep inside me was moved. Those men walking the beaches of Normandy were no different from my dad. I knew that my dad had held some bad memories for 50 years. I wanted him to be healed and I thought it might take revisiting Okinawa and Sugar Loaf Hill to do it.

After Peter Jennings' show, I called Dad. He had watched the same show on ABC. I could also tell by the sound of his voice that he had had his evening Johnny Walker Red.

At the end of our conversation, I asked Dad if there were a 50th anniversary commemorative tour to Okinawa, would he go with me. I remember his answer. It was very subdued, but he said yes. Almost a surrender that he would be willing and ready to face his demons and attain what my sister would later call "closure" on that part of his life.

I recall hanging up, partially excited about the prospects and a little worried Dad would wake up the next day and find some excuse to cancel. Of course, at the time I didn't know if there would be any tour at all.

Little did I know what adventure had just begun; an odyssey that would take my dad and me 18,000 miles on four Pacific islands, and finally to Washington, D.C. Countless hours of phone conversations between Dad and me began that undoubtedly began to annoy my immediate and extended family. The research included equally countless hours of reading, letter correspondence, phone interviews and my first fax sent. The year of preparation may have begun that night, June 6, 1994, but Roger Jamieson's story begins much earlier.

PART I:

Scotland, Sandlots and Sugar Loaf

853 East 24th Street, Paterson, New Jersey, birthplace
and home of Roger Jamieson

East 24th Street Gang: From left; Jack Lee, Don Hall, Roger and
Clark Merselis

Roger Jamieson, May 1928

"I knew Roger for as early as human memory permits and we maintained a close friendship for as long as life permitted. We, as well as the rest of the neighborhood boys, were raised with good morals and principles and I don't remember any of us doing anything really bad—but we did have fun."

Donald Hall, lifelong friend of Roger Jamieson

CHAPTER 2

Humble Beginnings

I have never been to Scotland, but I am a Jamieson and of Scottish heritage. I am proud of that heritage. I am not certain exactly why I am so proud of this except I probably caught that from my father as he did from his father, whose father and mother actually had lived in Scotland. I liked the bagpipes, the concept of haggis and the kilts, William Wallace and the Highlanders, Braveheart, Highlander games, valiant stubborn warriors and so on. When I was a young boy, I loved watching a 1955 British movie called Wee Geordie, about a Scottish boy who becomes an Olympic hammer thrower.

I had a patient about my age in my medical practice who was from Scotland and had a beautiful brogue. I would talk to him about Scotland like I knew what I was talking about. One day he turned to me and said, "Jamieson, you're nothin' but a Scottish wannabee!" And although I was initially taken aback, I replied, "You know, you are right, I am three generations from Scotland. I have never been there. I am one quarter Scottish, one quarter Irish, one quarter Welsh and one quarter German. I am an American mongrel..." We both laughed. But even so, someday I would like to go visit the land of my ancestors.

Roger's great grandfather, James J. Jamieson, was born in 1836 in Scotland and later immigrated to New York City. While in Scotland he met and married Anna Morris on April 23, 1853 in the town of Liff Benvie and Invergowrie in the County of Angus, just west of Dundee, Scotland. James J. was an engineer and in business in New York City. The couple had three children, James, who was born on November 12, 1857 in New York City and two younger daughters, Jessie and Jean. James J. traveled to Cuba to install a new pump that he had invented. On the way home, on ship, James contracted Yellow Fever, died and was buried at sea. Family records reveal that the pump that James J. invented was not patented, so no financial benefit was given to the widow or her family. Anna took her three young children back to Scotland and lived there for 8 years. One of her deceased husband's coworkers back in New York City, James C. Young, recently widowed, wrote Anna and proposed marriage. She returned to New York City with her three children and married Mr. Young.

Roger's grandfather, James A., grew up to be an excellent baseball player during the infancy years of the sport. He had played with the legendary John McGraw. He was asked to be on the first organized professional baseball team in New York City. His stepfather and mother, James and Anna Young, however, being very good and strict Scottish Presbyterians, would not let him play as the league played on Sundays. (You might recall a similar story in the movie, *Chariots of Fire*, when in 1924, Eric Liddell, the Flying Scotsman, would not allow himself to compete on Sunday in the Olympics because of his strict adherence to this edict.) At any rate, James' parents not allowing him to play was a great disappointment to him.

Family history does not tell why James A. moved from New York City to Paterson, New Jersey, but one can imagine that the two cities being only twenty miles apart and Paterson having a large Scottish community with a Presbyterian church, James must have had some connection there. Most likely it was a job at the Rogers Locomotive Company that drew him to Paterson. James met and married Agnes Devine. She was an emigrant from Blairgowrie, Scotland. She was born in Rattray, Perth, Scotland on July 9, 1859 which is located just across the Ericht River from Blairgowrie. In the mid 1800s, this small village northwest of Dundee (birthplace of her parents) was a bustling center of flax and jute mills. Family history alludes to the fact that she probably worked the mills there and at age eleven was working the flax/silk mills in Paterson. The two were married at the home of David B. and Margaret Robertson Devine's (her parents) at 90 Spruce Street, with David Magic officiating. The marriage was recorded at the First Presbyterian Church.[1]

James held many positions of employment. In the family history I found, he is listed as an Iron Molder and then a laborer for the Paterson City Park, where he was a lamp lighter. I had heard he was a part-time fireman and a bartender, where he got the nick name Jimmy "Scoop Nickels" Jamieson for the rapid manner in which he could take the nickels off the bar on beer sales.

The couple had ten children. Roger's father, Walter, was number seven. The closest brother in age and friendship was Charles (Chuck), two years his elder. All the Jamieson boys were taught to play baseball by their father.

With so many mouths to feed, the children were needed to help support the family. Walter Jamieson, who finished his formal schooling after eighth grade, had several jobs. He and his brother William operated a grocery store in Paterson and then a deli in nearby Radburn, New Jersey. Walter then became a salesman for Ribbon and Ticker Paper Company, which sold Scott Paper products.

Thanks to the encouragement of his father, his main avocation and love was baseball, playing it in church leagues and semi-pro as well as coaching a top semi-pro team in Northern New Jersey, the Chevrolet Red Sox. Walter, with the help of his brother, Robert, started organized youth baseball in Paterson.

Walter Roger Jamieson, my father, was born on June 18, 1921, at his home at 853 East 24th St., Paterson, New Jersey. He was the first born child of Walter and Mary "Mae" Jamieson. He was known to his family and friends as Roger to distinguish him from his father, Walter. Mae Bullock Jamieson was a petite woman; she might have been 4-foot-10 and weighed a little over 100 pounds. She carried a strong punch and an even heavier purse. (Growing up I was taught to never look in a ladies purse. Hers was twenty pounds easy. I never did find out until recently that what was weighing down her purse was all of her jewelry. She carried it everywhere she went.) She was a trained singer and could play the piano. She was a high school graduate and never learned to drive. She taught Sunday school at the Church of the Messiah Presbyterian Church in Paterson. Grandma Jamieson loved her children and grandchildren and was very loving and affectionate. If, however, somebody crossed her or one of her own, she had no problem speaking her mind with a fiery outburst. She ran the family with an iron fist.

Paterson, New Jersey, was a multi-ethnic industrial town. Italians, Polish, Irish, German, Dutch, Eastern European and Scots blended together. Most of the African-Americans lived down by the river, on the West side near downtown and the mills, although some were integrated in other neighborhoods throughout Paterson. Walter and Mae lived in a modest, three bedroom cookie cutter house in a middle-class neighborhood. The silk industry was a major contributor to the local economy at that time.

Roger grew up and played with neighborhood friends. Don Hall, John and Clark Merselis, Jack Lee and a kid known as Fat Elvin comprised the East 24th Street Gang. Roger, from the stories I have heard was the ring leader. Roger was all boy; bright, adventurous, a planner and mischievous.

Don Hall, his lifelong friend lived directly across the street. East 24th Street was a through street and had considerable traffic. Don recalls that early on, Roger showed up at Don's side of the street unaccompanied. Don's mother questioned his presence and he replied, "I'm three and I can handle it." Roger's mother soon came across the street and took him home by the ear.

Another story that Don recalled involved a game they played. (Remember, these were the days without T.V., Gameboy, X-Box, computers, Wii or text messaging. All a kid had were his friends, a ball and imagination.) Don and Roger had a baseball game they played bouncing a tennis ball against the front steps of the house. A good hit on the point of the steps sent the ball into the street for a double, triple, etc. Roger's house had wooden steps and he would throw the ball against them for hours, driving his mother wild from the noise. He would catch it from her then.

One day, in retribution, Don found Roger stringing a long clothesline across the driveway, back and forth. Don recalls, "He told me his plan was to go to his back door and tease his mother until she ran after him, as she sometimes did. He would then hurdle the ropes and she would get stopped. I could not recall if the plan was successful, but it was a novel idea. Your dad was always a planner."

Behind Roger's home was undeveloped commercial property known by the neighborhood kids as "the lots". One day, the gang gathered discarded Christmas trees from all around and made a huge fire. Mr. Knox, the property owner, came along and demanded to know who was responsible for this activity. Roger stepped forward and said, "We are the originals." Mr. Knox grabbed him and the rest of the gang came to his rescue. There was much scuffling but, according to Don, it did not amount to much and there were no consequences.

Every day was another adventure. One day the boys rigged toy pistols to shoot BBs. They attempted to hit some delivery horses stationed in Mr. Knox's rented garage space. No horse was hit but the boys had fun trying.

There was no organized youth baseball in those days. For years, during the spring and summer months, Walter Jamieson would pack all of the available kids in his Oakland sedan (the record was 14) and take them to Eastside Park for makeshift baseball games and the occasional ice cream cone.

The milkman would come by daily in those days by horse-drawn carriage. I am sure Roger saw this day in and day out for years. Roger would have been about ten years old when one day he decided to show off to the neighborhood boys and jumped on the wagon while the milkman was delivering milk at the back side of his house. Once the horse sensed someone was on the cart, it signaled to him it was time to go to the next stop, so the horse took off with Roger in the driver's seat and the neighborhood kids watching in shock and awe, cheering him on and chasing after the runaway wagon. Roger panicked a bit and grabbed the reins to stop the horse. The horse now sensing something was wrong, realized that the milkman was not at the reigns and panicked, taking off faster down the street, heading full-speed toward an intersection. Jack Lee was heard yelling, "Hold the reins, Roggie. Hold the reins!" The horse turned a hard left at the intersection and then stopped at the curb. Eventually, the milkman caught up with the carriage and delivered Roger back to his mother.

In another incident, Roger's father started up his car in the garage to warm it up. Roger's mother was on the phone talking to one of her friends. Roger got in the car with the folding garage door partially open, put the car in reverse, and plowed the car through the door.

His mother, Mae, noting the incident, told her friend "… I have to say goodbye, Roger just drove the car through the garage."

Roger had two younger sisters, Lois and Marilyn. Family gatherings would find Roger playing with one of his favorite cousins, David Dougherty, son of David and Agnes (Jamieson) Dougherty. David, being an only child, and Roger, having no brothers, naturally gravitated towards each other at these family gatherings. They would become as Roger would say later, "Thick as brothers." David was about three years younger than Roger. According to a younger cousin, Donald Jamieson, David was an outgoing popular student at Hawthorne High and treated his younger cousins with kindness. Both he and his younger cousin John Jamieson recall David willing to play basketball with them at family gatherings. David had a hoop rigged up on the garage. All the younger cousins looked up to David. Roberta McCarthy remembers that David had his own radio in his bedroom and would allow the cousins to come in and listen to "The Shadow" or "Green Hornet" radio shows. David was a star athlete in basketball at Hawthorne High. In his senior year he was voted "King of the Campus". He was popular with the girls and had a special friend named Laura Minick from Clifton, New Jersey. After high school David got a job as a delivery boy for a popular local florist, McFarland's. Donald recalls that when he had a delivery in Paterson, David would pick him up for the ride. This was big doings for the younger cousin back in the early 1940s.

One family gathering occurred when Roger was 13. Like all good Presbyterian boys, he was forced to attend confirmation classes at The 2nd Presbyterian Church. The large, extended Jamieson family attended there; aunts, uncles, and numerous cousins. The weekly confirmation classes lasted about a month and usually occurred on Sunday afternoon, interfering with a boy's free play time. The climax was a confirmation ceremony. The large extended Jamieson Clan was there in full force to witness this coming of age event. There was only one problem: Roger was a no show. He had left and had decided that he wasn't going to sign up to be a Presbyterian quite yet. When he got home, the phone rang and it was one of his aunts calling for him. She wanted to know why he didn't get confirmed. He began to explain to his aunt that he was feeling pressured to commit and it was something that he was not really ready to commit to, so he didn't.

The aunt started lecturing her nephew when Grandma Jamieson got on the phone, a bit fired up, and said, "If the boy isn't ready, he isn't ready, and that's that," and hung up.

This told me something about Roger. He was nobody's lackey. He was an independent leader and thinker. These traits would carry him through life's challenges.

Roger was academically sharp. He attained a straight A average but consistently had unsatisfactory grades in conduct (he was the class clown). He attended P.S. 13 before matriculating to high school. He was a gaunt, short, scrappy and quippy freshman when he entered East Side High School in Paterson. He and two of his classmates, Myrene Garbaccio and Betty Alexander, all competed during his four years for top grades in college preparatory classes. Betty came from P.S. 25 in a slightly higher socio-economic section of Paterson. Her father, William E., was a drafting and shop teacher at Eastside High. Myrene, a transfer student, described herself as a "naïve country kid from Warren Point". She walked into huge Eastside High with fear and trembling. The first two kids she met were Betty and Roger in English I. They helped her diagram a sentence, something she had not been taught in rural Warren Point. Roger helped her with Latin and she helped him with science. A competitive friendship and rivalry developed over those years and a lot of banter between Roger, Myrene, and Betty ensued; part flirtation and part battle of the sexes.

In Roger's, Betty's and Myrene's sophomore year, they signed up for 'Miss Ryan's Dancing Class'. My guess is that Gramma Mae signed Roger up and he had no choice. The boys lined up on one side and the girls on the other. The gentlemen were in shirts, ties and jackets; the ladies in dresses, stockings, heels and white gloves. After dance lessons, Roger, Betty and Myrene would go to Hashagens Soda Shoppe for coffee milk shakes. Myrene's father would wait outside before driving the girls home and Roger was left to walk back to East 24th Street by himself.

It was coming time to graduate and Roger had an almost perfect GPA. He was definitely college material, but this was 1938, eight years into the Great Depression, and his father was looking forward to his son taking a job and assisting in the family's financial welfare. Paying out for college was a waste of money by Grandpa Jamieson's notion.

Uncle Al and Aunt Jessie (Jamieson) King were aware of Roger's potential and knew of Walter's reluctance to encourage Roger in going to college. Al King, an educator and coach at nearby Hawthorne High, and a strong-willed personality, had a visit with Walter and Mae and insisted that Roger must go to college. (Note: This was not the only nephew Uncle Al went to bat for. Donald Jamieson relayed to me a similar incident. When he was eighteen he landed a job as a ship's purser and was making a good wage. After his first cruise, Uncle Al convinced young Don to go to college. He ended up at Farleigh Dickenson University and graduated with a degree in accounting). After some haranguing, my grandparents gave in. Roger ended up at Muhlenberg College, a Lutheran school, in Allentown, Pennsylvania. With some scholarship money and a waiting job in the dorm dining hall, and with help from his parents, Roger scraped through four years of college. He would come home in the summers and his father would ask him what classes he was taking. "Philosophy." he would respond. Grandpa would ask, "How's that going to help you get a job?" Dad would try to explain, but Grandpa Jamieson didn't fully grasp the concept and benefit of a liberal arts college education. Over time, however, he did see it was the right thing for his son to be doing.

Roger thrived in the college environment. He and his four-year dorm roommate, Ed Robertson, caused enough mischief at Muhlenberg to get them both expelled (if they ever got caught). An example of one of their college pranks was when they decided to take a toilet stall door off its hinges one late Friday night. They thought it would be fun to drop it down the open stairwell from the third floor to the first floor. That would make a loud noise and wake everybody up! Fun, right?

So they quietly made their way out of the bathroom with the stall door in hand to the stairwell. They positioned the door and let it drop and the door landed not on the floor but on the first-floor banister, taking it completely out and then making a loud noise, waking everyone up. Ed and Roger quickly dashed into their room, shut the door, and went to sleep. Half the dorm was up mulling the situation. Although suspected, the two never got caught. (Parenthetically, I might add that Ed Robertson more than paid back Muhlenberg for the damages done, when he and his wife Lois donated funds for a new dormitory later on.)

Roger was also the editor of the college paper and captain of his baseball team. He excelled in English and developed an affection for pipe-smoking. Life was good in 1941 for Roger. Studies, baseball, dances and college antics kept him occupied.

The attack on Pearl Harbor on December 7, 1941, in his senior year, changed everything. Plans for teaching English would be put on hold but he decided to finish college before enlisting. At the urging of his father, Roger enlisted with the United States Marine Corps on April 7, 1942, at the Philadelphia Naval Yard. Grandpa Jamieson, a World War I Army sergeant with no combat experience, had heard about the Marines. He heard they were the best fighting unit around, so he wanted his son to join the best. Officers' Candidate School would start on August 11, 1941. Roger graduated from college in June and then prepared for war.

David Dougherty followed his Cousin Roger's lead and joined the Marines as an enlisted man after he graduated from high school. According to Cousin Donald, "With David in the Marines, my visits to Aunt Aggie and Uncle Dave's were quiet to say the least." There was a tension there with their only child heading for war.

And Donald noted that Paterson, New Jersey responded to the attack. William E. Alexander, Betty's father and a World War I Navy veteran, upon hearing the news of Pearl Harbor, his Irish blood boiling, marched down to the Naval Headquarters office at 19 Church Street in New York City and requested a commission. He was denied due to his age.

Rationing gasoline and sugar, leather and even ice cream became the norm. Car headlights had to be half masked so they would not emit too much light at night. Every neighborhood had air raid wardens. Practice blackouts were run by the wardens. In Donald Jamieson's neighborhood was an anti-aircraft battery and searchlight crew. Wright's Aircraft replaced silk as the main industry with several plants working around the clock seven days a week. They assembled aircraft engines. Several family members worked shifts, including my Grandmother Jamieson who packed propellers. Paterson sent their young men to fight and those that remained behind supported the war effort with sacrifice and work.

From left, Lt. Rex Dillow and Lt. Roger Jamieson

Roger as Marine baseball player, Camp Pendleton, 1943

"As iron sharpens iron, so one man sharpens another.

Proverbs 27:17 NIV

"I have never had a bad day on Hawaii...this is still the best duty in the South Pacific."

Roger Jamieson, 1995

"If there is such a thing as God's "Universal All Star Team", there surely is a spot for a sure handed, slap hitting, speedy second baseman, a Marine, a great father and husband, a man who always seemed to say, and more importantly , to do the right thing."

Doug Jamieson, son, from his eulogy to Dad, June 15, 2007.

CHAPTER 3

Rex Dillow, Hawaii and Baseball

Baseball, the American pastime, came into its own in the early 20th century. As mentioned in the last chapter, my great-grandfather, James A. Jamieson, son of Scottish immigrants, loved the game. His wife, Agnes, did not. She viewed it from the seamy side, associating it with gambling and general rowdiness. And there definitely was that element and thus the reputation was not necessarily undeserved. I am sure there was some tension between the two as James taught his six boys to play: James, Robert, William, Charles, Walter and David. Growing up in Northern New Jersey in the early 1900s, the boys played team sports including basketball and even church league bowling, but baseball was their favorite and they played it at every opportunity. My grandfather, aside from his skills at playing, developed a keen mind for the strategy of the game. He was also well known in the region for memorizing professional baseball statistics and would be called on regularly to clarify a question about someone's record.

Most boys of that era in Paterson, New Jersey were lucky to finish eighth grade. They were expected to find a job to help support their family. Charlie Jamieson, Roger's uncle, was 15 years old in 1908, when he started pitching for the Patterson Lafayettes, a top semi-professional team. He had already worked his way up to a silk factory foreman by age 17; in charge of 28 men and 14 women, but when the factory shift whistle blew, he was off to the sandlots. In 1912, when Charlie was 19, he signed with the Buffalo Bisons of the International League. A pitcher on the team, and Paterson neighbor, George Merritt, saw him playing in Paterson and recruited him. Charlie signed for $250 a month. By the end of that summer, Merritt lost his pitching job and Charlie became his replacement. Three years later at the age of 22, Charlie was sold to the Washington Senators. He played with the great pitcher, Walter Johnson. Charlie had transitioned to batter/fielder and learned a lot about Walter Johnson's pitching secrets, which he remembered and used successfully when facing him after being traded. After a short stint with the Philadelphia Athletics, the owner, Cornelius McGillicuddy, (Connie Mack) traded him to the Cleveland Indians in 1919. This trade goes down as one of the top ten best trades the Cleveland Indians organization ever made.[2] Connie Mack would later say of the trade, "...One of the worst mistakes I ever made in my career was when I traded Charley Jamieson to the Cleveland Indians in 1919." Charlie was glad to be traded as he had once characterized the Athletics' owner as "pretty tight with that dollar".

The move turned out to be the break he needed. Charlie started out as a utility player in the first year. During that season, in a crucial turn of events, the manager of the Indians, Lou Faul, decided in a late inning in a tight game against the Yankees to pitch to Babe Ruth rather than walk him. Babe knocked out the game winning three run homer for the Yanks. That night the Indian's owner fired Faul and Tris Speaker, the starting center fielder, was named player-manager. He called a team meeting and stated there would be some changes. One of them was "Jamieson is going to be my lead off hitter and starting left fielder". And Charlie remained the starter for the next 14 years. When he was let go, he was offered a managerial position with the Toledo Mud Hens which he turned down. He signed with Jersey City of the International League and five weeks into the season he fractured his ankle ending his professional career.

In 1920, he played an integral role in the Indians' World Series win against the Brooklyn Robins (Dodgers) batting .333. For most of the 1924 season, Charlie Jamieson led the American League in batting. He was hitting .384 when he broke his thumb in early September. No disabled list then, he kept playing and his average dropped to .359, finishing second that year to Babe Ruth (.378). Jamieson led the league in singles that season.

He was also an excellent fielder. It was said with Speaker in center and Jamieson in left, that portion of the field was impenetrable. In The Ballplayers,(1990) by Mike Shatzkin, it states," Defensively he made spectacular diving catches and powerful accurate throws. In 1928 his 22 outfield assists were tops, and in a 17 day span he started two triple plays. He is the only major league outfielder to ever do this. (*Editor's note: to this day, on occasion on June 9 in the sport's pages under "This Day in Sports..., there is mention of this fact.*) Jamieson was a frequent MVP candidate (and finished 3rd one season) though never a winner."[3] In May of 1969 The Cleveland Sports Press and the Indians organization released the results of a poll conducted to decide the All-Time Cleveland team. Charlie Jamieson was named as the All-Time Left fielder. And according to The Cleveland Indians Encyclopedia, "It was also said by many that Jamieson was the best player **not** in the Hall of Fame. ...Jamieson's lifetime batting of .303 is higher than 44 Hall of Famers."[4]

I have heard a series of stories about Charlie Jamieson relayed to me from Roger. On August 16, 1920, the Cleveland Indians were in New York playing the Yankees at the Polo Grounds. The Fireman's League of Paterson, N.J. was presenting Charlie with a diamond ring. Charlie had played baseball in the off season for them as a ringer under the name O'Reilly. At the end of the season, he donated his pay to the Widow's Fund. The Fireman presented Charlie with a diamond ring before the game. Charlie's mother Agnes, who was not a fan of the game, reluctantly consented to go to the game and brought one of her daughters, Sara, age 20. Charlie went 2 for 5 that game and the Indians won a close game 4-3.

But none of this compares to the real historical significance of this date in baseball. Carl Mays was pitching that day for the Yankees. The native Kentuckian was well known for his submarine (side arm) pitching technique. He also was a superb spitballer, which was legal then. The spitball, a scuffed ball thrown with licorice juice, or spit or tar on it would cause a baseball to make erratic movement on its way to the plate. Ray Chapman, also a native Kentuckian, was an up and coming star and the starting shortstop for the Indians. He batted in the number 2 spot behind the lead off batter, Charlie Jamieson. Ray was well known for crowding the plate and even placing his head in the strike zone. Batting helmets were not used. Ray leaned into the plate and Carl Mays let off a low rising spitball. Chapman stood in position and did not flinch. He may not have seen the ball rising on him. The ball hit Ray directly on the left temple making a cracking sound. He went down and the ball bounced back at Mays. Thinking the ball hit the end of the bat, according to the newspaper articles written, Mays picked the ball up and threw it to first for the out. He then saw that Ray Chapman was unconscious with blood coming out his ear canals. Ray was rushed to a local hospital and died after a surgeon's brave attempt to remove the skull fragments from Chapman's brain. Ray Chapman is the only major league baseball player ever to die playing the game. Agnes Jamieson, having viewed this tragic spectacle, had seen all she needed to see. This event reinforced her previously held beliefs about the game. She never attended another baseball game again. And according to John Jamieson, a son of Charlie, Agnes wanted him to quit playing ball right then. Thankfully, he didn't obey his mother.

Charlie Jamieson, who was in the dugout when this accident occurred, tells a different story about the fate of the ball. This information comes from an article written by Jack De Vries in 1997. The pitcher never picked up the ball. Charlie did when he ran out with the rest of the Indians to assist

Ray Chapman. Charlie put the ball in his pocket and after the game threw it in his bag and forgot about it until after the World Series. "I cleaned out my locker and brought the ball home. I never really wanted to look at it", Jamieson described. Jamieson gave the ball to Bob Curley, a local sportswriter and St. Luke's High School baseball coach in Ho Ho Kus, New Jersey. Curley used the ball at the team practice the next day for infield drills. A slow bouncer was hit to third; it took a bad hop and struck the player in the right eye, shattering his cheekbone. When the coach realized it was the Chapman ball, he retrieved it and locked it away. Curley eventually retired and moved to Florida. The ball has not been seen since Curley's death.[5]

In a post script, Carl Mays reported himself that evening to the District Attorney's office in New York and was cleared on any charges. He apologized for the accident.[6] Several major league players wanted him banned from the game. He was not banned, but was eventually traded away to the National League. Fans booed him whenever he would appear to pitch and he soon left the game a dejected man.

That year, the Cleveland Indians went on to win the World Series. All the players wore a black armband in honor of Ray Chapman. Mrs. Chapman received the $4000 bonus each player was given for winning the fall classic.

Rule changes linked to Ray Chapman's death included making spitballs illegal. The 17 pitchers currently in the league who made a living by this pitch were registered as such and were allowed to use the pitch until they retired. Another rule change involved umpires replacing scuffed balls with new ones. Wearing batting helmets became the rule much later. Major leaguers playing prior to the rule change could opt out from wearing a helmet if they chose.

In 1926, when Roger was a young boy of 5, his first childhood memory was being taken to Yankee Stadium by his father when his Uncle Chuck was in town playing against the Yankees. It was a simpler, less formal time then. Pre-game, my Grandfather Jamieson brought Roger down to the Cleveland dugout. Uncle Chuck picked him up and carried him over to the opposing field's dugout to meet one of his friends, Babe Ruth. Babe and Charlie were friends, professionally, both started out as pitchers and played the same position (Left Field) and even shared the same birthday. Their careers spanned the same time. Babe Ruth gave Charlie the nickname of "Cuckoo" for the way he would clown around in practice catching baseballs. In those days, an outfielder would leave his glove out on the field. Ruth would, on occasion, fill Charlie's glove with grass between innings.

Babe was, as we all know, a clown and attracted a large crowd wherever he went. He asked Roger what he wanted to be when he grew up.

Young Roger answered, "A baseball player!" "Well," the Babe replied, "don't get fat like me." The Babe let out a barrel laugh and the group of players all laughed with Babe. My dad never forgot that moment. He decided then and there that he would become a ball player. (If you would like to learn more about Charlie Jamieson's illustrous baseball career, you can log on at www.onceamarinebook.info and be linked to a PDF file.)

Roger grew up in this baseball culture, but by the time he entered high school he was small, kind of scrawny, yet scrappy and determined. His high school career was anything but stellar. He did not receive much encouragement from his father or the varsity coach at East Side High School in Paterson, New Jersey. Roger rode the pines for four years, but never quit. Roger went on to Muhlenberg College in Allentown, where eventually, in his junior year, he came of age and locked in a starting position at second base. As mentioned before, his senior year, he was the captain of the team. He was agile on the field, a good left-handed slap hitter with quick feet. He had matured into a great finesse baseball player.

I believe he wanted to prove to his father that he had the stuff and at the same time to show his Uncle Chuck that he could play. In his senior year, the Japanese attacked Pearl Harbor. Roger had heard of the Hawaiian Islands, but he had never heard of a place called Pearl Harbor. The war would force Roger and millions upon millions of other young men and women to put up their playthings for awhile. Roger hung up his cleats and with it, put his love for the game of baseball on hold. Duty called.

Roger's training career in the United States Marine Corps was a circuitous one. Entering Officers' Candidate School at Quantico, Virginia was no guarantee that he would automatically pass through. OCS was a screening process and in fact two months into training in October 1942, he washed out. The DI's and officers felt Roger was not serious enough and looked too young and immature to lead Marines. They probably were not incorrect in their assessment at the time. Roger was 5-foot-8, 140 pounds, had a light beard and a baby face. He also had the reputation his whole life of being a class clown (a trait I inherited). From what I gathered from conversations with him, is that he went into OCS with some of his college prankster mentality and it did not sit well with his trainers. OCS is a weeding-out process and he was weeded out.

He was called in and was informed he was washed out. This was a shock and embarrassment to him at the time. The commanding officer said Roger had two choices. He could find him a position in an Officers' Candidate School in the Army or he could appoint him a corporal and send him to Camp Lejeune, New River, North Carolina. Roger had been indoctrinated enough at OCS to know he would rather be an enlisted Marine than an Army officer, so off he went. By February 1943, his commanding officer, who had reviewed his file and knew his history, saw potential in him. Roger was promoted to sergeant and was transferred to Camp Pendleton, California. He was maturing and learning to lead men.

Roger now had a squad he trained. On the long trip by train from LeJeune to Pendleton, there were plenty of stops along the way. This was wartime and citizens were supportive and aware of the young men in the services. When the train full of Marines rolled into a small town in Texas, Sgt. Jamieson took his squad out of the train and called out a "close order drill" (precision march in columns) while the locals watched and cheered. He said he never felt more like a Marine as when he was barking commands to the men as they precisely followed his lead.

When he arrived at Camp Pendleton in Oceanside, California, he had some chances to play ball on base. Sometimes opposing teams fielded professional baseball players who had enlisted during the war. He found he loved the climate and the terrain in California; what a difference from New Jersey. Roger's horizons were expanding as he traveled to new places. He looked around and liked what he saw. He thought to himself that perhaps someday he would find a way to return to California to live.

In May 1943, while the war raged on in Europe and the Pacific, officers were being killed in great numbers. Replacements were needed. Someone had seen leadership potential in him, so Roger was ordered to Camp Elliott, just south, in La Jolla for officer screening class. This was a pre-OCS course to screen for potential officers. Dad had learned some lessons as a corporal and sergeant and he had matured over the last year and a half. He had also had time to reflect on his first wash out. He was selected to return to Quantico. This time it was all business. No jokes. No mistakes. He scored the highest marks to date on the machine-gun range. He passed through and was commissioned Second Lieutenant on 10 August 1943.

Roger was sent to Camp Lejuene again, this time in preparation for "permanent duty beyond the seas". It is here that Roger met fellow officers and tent mates Bill Phillips, Buck Osborne and Rex Dillow. They were assigned to a 10 week Rifle Platoon Leader's course. Rex said later that perhaps this was to keep them busy until the new draft was organized. The course consisted mostly of field exercises. The Officer-in-Charge, according to Dillow, was a captain and veteran of Guadacanal (suffice it to say a seasoned veteran). The training reflected lessons learned in that operation and it was assumed that the climate in North Carolina was similar to that of the South Pacific. They made landings on Onslow Beach at night, waded in waist deep water and sometimes in the snow (not exactly South Pacific balmy). They were not allowed to start a fire at night, lest they be "spotted by the enemy."

Dillow told me that he and Roger quickly became special friends, studying and working together as much as possible. He noted that the Officer–in-Charge had an obsession about "observing". His favorite expression was "you saw but you didn't observe" and he tried to develop an ability in the young officers and NCOs to record mental pictures of everything seen, which could then be recalled like memories. On conditioning marches and field exercises, the captain would call out individuals to give details of areas that they had passed. If the individual could not recall the detail, he would be sent back to get the answer. On one occasion, Roger was asked the color of the shutters on a house they passed, one of many. When he didn't answer correctly he double timed it back the half mile to find out. Roger noted, "Captain, in combat we will know what we are looking for. I have a problem visualizing the value, in a combat situation, of knowing the color of the shutters on a house". The class found it very amusing, the captain a little less so. (It seemed like some of Roger's class clowning was not yet extinguished.) But I will say that Roger knew that humor could get you through some of the stressful and tedious times in your life.

Rex and Roger were competitive friends. They both relayed a story to me separately about a wrestling match they had. One cold morning in the field the two young strong and energetic bucks got into a friendly and spirited discussion that evolved into a shoving match that soon escalated into a wrestling match. There they were, rolling around on the frozen turf while the rest of the class cheered them on. Roger told me he pinned Dillow. Rex's recollection was different; they never agreed who the winner was.

The camp was a preparation for shipping overseas. Marines were arriving in large numbers and there was an immediate need for Platoon leaders. Roger, Rex, Bill Phillips, Buck Osborne and 2 other officers occupied a 30 square foot hut: tight quarters and isolated from civilization. There was nowhere to go for leave. They were stuck in these shacks after hours and spent a lot of time together talking and arguing.

Rex relayed to me a typical incident. He noted that in giving commands to a platoon, the preparatory command, "platoon" is given; "Platoon—Attention, Platoon—Forward March". Drill commands are pretty much chopped up and can hardly be recognized by the untrained ear, but the preparatory command "platoon" is generally two syllables yelled out crisp and clear. Rex noted to the officers in the tent that Roger gave commands to his platoon with the preparatory command "toon". When Rex kidded Roger about this, Roger retorted, "Here is Rex marching his platoon" and then Roger gave out commands with a long drawn out

P L A T O O O O N" while marching back and forth in the little hut. Rex commented "I wanted to hit him!" But hey—what else was there to do in the middle of the woods? These men were a small part of a mammoth movement and the Marines were biding there time until it was their turn to go into combat.

Probably another time Rex wanted to deck Roger was when Roger would sing a parody he called "Sweet Rexy O'Dillow".

Buck Osborne was a university graduate, A Phi Beta Kappa, and by Rex Dillow's estimate "one of the most unorganized persons I had ever met". Rex notes Buck had at least 25 sets of underwear, due to forgetting to send his laundry out and needing to buy more. When it was time to pack to leave for overseas, Roger and Rex came back to the hut to find Buck's father and mother there with his mother sitting on the bunk packing his boy's trunk for war. This busted Rex and Roger up.

In late February 1944, the draft went by train to Norfolk where they embarked for Pearl Harbor via Panama. This would be the first of many boat rides to come. Two years after hearing of Pearl Harbor for the first time, Roger was now landing there and reporting to the First Provisional Marine Brigade. Hawaii was a training and holding ground for Navy, Army, and Marines heading out to battle in the South and Central Pacific. By now, in 1944, the Marines had taken Guadalcanal, Tarawa, and the Marshall Islands.

Unbeknownst to Roger, his cousin David Dougherty had returned to Maui from his first battle, helping to take Roi Namur, in the Marshall Islands while with the Fourth Marine Division. David had contracted dysentery after the battle and was recuperating in a naval hospital in Honolulu, separated temporarily from his squad who were training at Camp Maui on the north side upland in Maui, an absolutely beautiful location for R&R. Many of the Fourth Marine Division veterans have commented of their wonderful days and great memories on Maui and taking leave at Lahaina.

One day on base, Roger heard about a Marine baseball team being formed, and he went over to the captain who was managing the team. He had barely picked up a ball in a year or so, but he pleaded with the coach to try out (apparently the team had already been selected). After some cajoling by Roger, the captain agreed to give him a tryout. He pitched Roger a few balls, which he missed, then shanked, but then with the cobwebs dusted off, Roger began connecting to left, then to right. The coach had seen enough and ordered Roger to the field. He hit him grounders and he scooped everything up in sight. The captain had seen enough, called him in, told him he had made the team, and gave him a fresh baseball uniform, cleats and all. This would be a traveling team. Roger was ecstatic and came back to the tent. There was Lieutenant Rex Dillow waiting. "What's the uniform, Jamie?" Rex knew of Roger's great love for baseball. He knew Roger was a diehard NY Giants fan. Over the last several months, they had many hours of down time to talk about memorable occasions. Roger had relayed to Rex that he was at the Polo Grounds for the 1934 All Star Game where Giant's Carl Hubbell struck out 5 of the all time great hitters in a row; Babe Ruth, Lou Gehrig, Jimmie Foxx, Al Simmons and Joe Cronin. Rex knew about Roger's Uncle Charlie Jamieson. And Rex remembered that Roger had admitted to him once that he had an obsession to play 2nd base for the Giants. So Roger explained to Rex that he had just tried out and made the traveling baseball team. He would be reassigned to a position of officer in charge of the mess hall and play baseball while the war raged on. Rex was less than impressed. "So that's why you joined the Marines, Jamieson? …. to play baseball?" Rex was very critical of Roger's decision and stated he had a problem with anyone joining the Marine Corps and then volunteering to play baseball in wartime. Roger mounted a small verbal response, noting that several major leaguers would be playing in the Hawaiian League, but it was over—end of discussion. He returned to his cot, lay down, and stared at the ceiling and thought real hard. What a dream, to play baseball and travel. But Rex's words convicted him and pricked his conscience deeply. Torn between his love for baseball and the reality of what was going on in the world, he resigned to the truth. He got up, carried his baseball uniform to the captain that selected him and told the captain thanks, but he hadn't joined the Marines to play baseball. He received some chiding from the captain but it was done.

Roger was forever grateful to Rex Dillow that day for confronting him with the truth. Roger joined to fight the war. The cleats were hung up again. Later in life the two would meet again and Roger thanked his World War II buddy for "setting me straight and keeping me from doing something I'm sure I would have later regretted." Iron had sharpened iron again. And that is exactly what real friends are for.

The Paterson connection: From Left: Roger and Marvin Pike on Guam, August 1944

CHAPTER 4

Guadalcanal, Guam, Guadalcanal and Ulithi

In late March 1944, Roger and Rex Dillow were both assigned to the First Provisional Marine Brigade, then on Guadalcanal in the Solomon Islands. They shipped off from Pearl Harbor and at some point on their journey crossed the Equator. They participated in the Navy's "Crossing the Line" initiation, complete with tributes to King Neptune.

Upon arrival to Guadalcanal, Roger was assigned to brigade headquarters as a liaison officer. Rex Dillow was assigned to headquarters, but soon thereafter was reassigned as a platoon leader in the 22nd Marine Regiment after a lieutenant had drowned. The brigade was in its final stages of preparations for the recapture of Guam, which was the first American possession seized by the Japanese 3 years earlier.

Roger was a coding officer. One of his assignments was to help screen the thousands of letters being written and shipped home to family and friends. By the time most recipients got a letter from their Marine several weeks would have passed. The letter more resembled a slice of Swiss cheese after the coding officer had removed any information that could be considered classified. Even though the Marines had been warned about leaking sensitive information such as location and possible assignment, several tried to sneak hints to family. Here's one Roger read while stationed in Hawaii. "Say hello to Aunt Pearl and Uncle Harbor." That wasn't too subtle. One in Guadalcanal went like this: "I can't tell you the canal we are stationed at, but what a canal!" I guess you can't really blame the troops for trying, but as the old World War II saying went, "Loose lips sink ships."

The First Provisional Marine Brigade shipped off from Guadalcanal and held off the Eniwetok Atoll. They were planning on landing on Guam on June 15, 1944. Initial reconnaissance revealed that the stronghold of the Marianas Islands was Guam and a weaker force was to be found on Saipan and Tinian. That intelligence proved to be incorrect. It took 3 weeks to clear the Japanese off of Saipan and then Tinian. It was discovered on landing that Saipan was much more heavily occupied than thought, so the First Provisional Marine Brigade floated back and forth in the Central Pacific to and from Eniwetok Atoll for 10 days waiting for Saipan to be secured. Roger recalls that the armada would shove off and some time in the middle of the night would turn and return back to the Eniwetok Atoll region. The men never got off the ship and they were never told the logic behind the turn-arounds. In total, before the Marines landed on Guam, they had been at sea for 35 consecutive days.

With Saipan and Tinian captured, the First Provisional Marine Brigade finally headed toward Guam. Roger was assigned to headquarters communications as a coding officer. He landed in the 6th wave; most of the initial onshore battle was over, but this was, in fact, his first exposure to war. He landed on what was called White Beach, a few miles west of the town of Agat. He remembers seeing a tall soldier running across the beach but didn't realize that this was a Japanese soldier. Before he could pull his gun, a more experienced Marine shot him down. Roger was assigned by Brigadier General Lemuel C. Shepherd to be his personal liaison officer to the 77th Army Division, which was in reserve. Major General Bruce was the Army commander. Roger did discuss with his G-1 Major Overstreet that he did want the assignment, and wondered why he had been chosen. Lemuel Shepherd stated that Roger was an athlete and was fast.

In Roger's own words, he stated, "Although I was not responsible for winning any battles on Guam, probably because the brigade made it unnecessary for the 77th to be deployed, I found the duty satisfying since I did get a feeling that I was doing something positive. I was on call around the clock for approximately 2 weeks, or in other words, until the 3rd of August, at which point mopping up started and I was then assigned to liaison with the 3rd Marine Division. During the above-mentioned 2 weeks, I ate and slept either at the brigade or at the 77th command post, wherever I was. Each general would send a runner for me, sometimes in the middle of the night, and off I would go to the other headquarters. There was more dark time than daylight duty, since our enemy seemed to like to charge after happy hour. On a couple of occasions, at night when I was near the battle lines, I had to hit the deck and creep or crawl until things settled down.

"I was sent to the 3rd Marine Division just once and was then hospitalized because of dengue fever. (Editor's note: *This mosquito-borne viral infection, also known as break- bone fever, wracks the entire body with pain and fever. After about a week the fever breaks, rendering the person generally fatigued, weak, and depressed with no appetite for about a month.*) This, plus some jungle rot I got several days after the Guam landing because of no chance to wash, shave, and change clothes, constituted my sufferings on Guam. By chance, I bumped into an acquaintance from Paterson, N.J. at the 77th headquarters, which was a break because he was the lieutenant in charge of a photography unit consisting of him plus a sergeant and a corporal, and they had better chow than we did at our headquarters. He was Marvin Pike, a sports reporter on the Paterson Morning Call, and he knew me because he had often covered the Chevrolet Red Sox. I had a picture of him and me on Guam. He wanted to send the picture and story on me to the Call from Guam, but I persuaded him not to do it. My feeling was that there were too many real heroes, and many of them dead, getting nothing for their efforts."

During the cleanup operation of Guam in August 1944, Roger received a letter from his father that David Dougherty was declared Missing in Action June 15, 1944 on Saipan. He also received a letter from David's mother, Aunt Aggie, who was concerned that David might have been taken prisoner and wondered if Roger could find out what was going on. Dad wrote back that he would look into it, but kept to himself the reality that at this point in the war, the Japanese Army was not taking any prisoners. Roger made some inquiries, but did not get much useful information.

Roger was washed out by the disease, which landed him in sick bay. Word got to him that his First Provisional Marine Brigade was heading back to Guadalcanal. He would have to stay behind to recuperate. He didn't want to separate from his brigade, so he requested to leave. He was told that if he could physically pull himself up the cargo nets onto the transport ship, he could go. He mustered every last ounce of strength to get himself and his pack up and over. A fellow Marine pulled him up and over the last rung. He lay on the deck absolutely exhausted as the ship departed. He made his way to sick bay and an orderly gave him an orange. Roger recalled it tasting so good, and it was his first sign of recovery. The troop ship steamed south to the Solomon Islands. It was typhoon season in the South and Central Pacific. There were the occasional rough seas where men lay in cots, seasick for days. When landing on Guadalcanal, the First Provisional Marine Brigade was then commissioned to the 6th Marine Division. This would become the only Marine division to be commissioned and decommissioned overseas. During Roger's stay in Guadalcanal, which lasted this time from the fall of 1944 to the spring of 1945, he was promoted to first lieutenant. Although he, like most Marines, was not privy to the details of the next assault, they trained for months.

Rex Dillow also returned from Guam, having also recovered from dengue fever. Here are his recollections. "After Guam, I returned to Guadalcanal where Roger and I were in tent camps several miles apart. The six-month training period before Okinawa was very pleasant and memorable. The brigade was expanded into the 6th Marine Division. All units had comfortable camps; regular supplies of good food, officers' clubs, and outdoor movies every night, and a Sunday baseball league. I saw Roger frequently; we met at officers' clubs, occasionally went to the movies together, and just visited. The incident on Guadalcanal I remember most vividly involved a baseball game. Roger and I each managed a baseball team in the Sunday league. I think we both anticipated our scheduled meetings more than any other game. It was played on Roger's home field and was undoubtedly one of the sloppiest games I have ever seen, but my team won. I don't think Roger ever forgot it. Of course, I probably wasn't a very gracious winner."

Rex and Roger would continue to train and they saw each other one more time just before they embarked for Okinawa. They would be separated at that point for 50 years.

One thing Roger talked about was the fact that a few Marines committed suicide. The reasons varied; perhaps a Dear John letter but more commonly despair, burnout, and depression were the root causes. There was a belief amongst many Marines that if you had survived two landings, your number was up on the third. Many of these Marines had battled and survived two landings and had not been home for well over a year. Roger recalls that, unlike the Navy and the Army, the Marines Corps did not easily give leave. Roger felt that the policy was brutally harsh. A typical way a Marine would commit suicide was drowning. The Marine would swim out into the surrounding lagoon and drown. He would have tied a rope around his leg so that the body could be retrieved. Family members would be told that their son died heroically in battle. There was no 24/7 "drive-by media" covering this and if there were an embedded reporter, he would keep it confidential.

Another story Roger related to me was how officers were treated better than the enlisted. Roger did not agree with that. One afternoon, Roger came back to his barracks to find an enlisted man rummaging through a fellow officer's trunk. Officers were given bottled alcohol; enlisted were not. The enlisted man had his hands on a bottle when Roger confronted him. A tussle broke out and Roger held the scrappy young Marine down until MPs could arrest him. Later, Roger did not want to testify against him, knowing that the young man would be court-martialed and sent home to jail and disgrace. "All the kid wanted was a drink, just like the officers," Roger recalled. Roger decided not to testify against him. Then Roger was told by his commanding officer that he would be court-martialed if he didn't testify. So reluctantly he obeyed, and the young man's fate was sealed. Roger later reminiscing about this event, sadly wondered whatever happened to that young man. He regretted the incident. I suggested that perhaps Roger had saved his life.

On the lighter side, Roger recalled an outdoor movie theater that was set up for enlisted and officers. It was an open-air theater and sometimes it would pour rain during the movies. Favorite movies to see were recent war morale boosters starring the likes of John Wayne. These movies were created to boost the morale of the people back home. Likewise, it was thought that servicemen overseas would be encouraged by the battlefield bravado of the Duke. Morale was boosted — but for the wrong reasons. The raucous crowd comments mocking John Wayne caused more entertainment than the movie itself.

On a side note, I read in George Fiefer's book, Tennozan that the Duke showed up at a Naval Hospital in Hawaii to pay a visit to the wounded Marines. John Wayne wore a fancy cowboy suit, spurs and a pistol and went around greeting the wounded. He was received initially with "stony silence" then someone booed and the whole ward started booing him.[7]

After several months of training, the Marines shipped off in March and headed north to a new assignment. More and more ships were met along the way. They all congregated on a small atoll called Ulithi Atoll on the island of Mog Mog in the Central Western Pacific. This would be a final resting point before landing on Okinawa. All Marines were given two beers and a chicken sandwich. The entire event was a pressure release before the big battle. They could swim, play baseball or volleyball and generally have a rowdy good time. Roger saw one or two men fall off ships that day and die when landing on pylons. The scene is described in Tennozan. These are quotes from Marines: "There were battleships, cruisers, more cruisers - you wouldn't believe it," one said. "We were in the middle of a phenomenal amount of floating iron," and "Just for the hell of it - or to convince myself I wasn't dreaming - I started counting the ships. It was impossible; too many of them, just too unbelievably many," and "I felt myself smiling inside. Maybe I'd be hit on this Okinawa where we were going, but there was no way we could lose with that incredible number of ships."[8] With the party over, the ships reloaded and headed north to Okinawa.

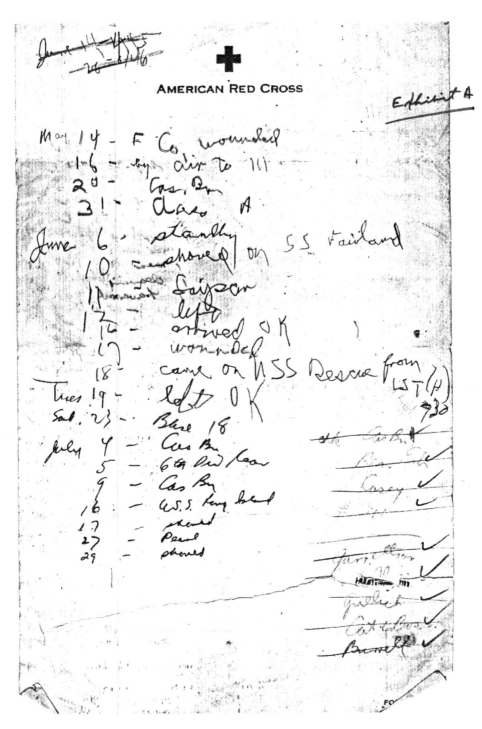

Lt. Roger Jamieson's diary from May 14-July 29, 1945

"I never met a braver man. When I asked him where that bravery came from, Dad said, 'Jay, they already tried to kill me twice, what else can they do to me?'

from my eulogy to my father, June 15, 2007

CHAPTER 5

In His Own Words- Okinawa

Somewhere in the Western Central Pacific after one last blowout party on Ulithi Atoll of Mog Mog, it was announced that the next landing would be Okinawa, an island south of the main islands of Japan proper. As Rex Dillow put it recently, "By this time the Japanese high command recognized that they could not win the war, so their objective was to make the operation so costly as to dissuade the U.S. from invading the home islands and perhaps obtain a negotiated peace." The battle plan for Okinawa by the Japanese command was that of a battle of attrition; dig in, entrench and slow the forward progress of the American fighting machine and in the process make the victory so costly that the Americans would negotiate.

It is not the purpose of this book to adequately cover the Battle of Okinawa. That has already been done by various authors including Okinawa: Touchstone to Victory by Frank M. Benis, Tennozan by George Feifer, Killing Ground on Okinawa: The Battle for Sugar Loaf Hill by James Hallis, and a recent book that I have not had the privilege of reading called The Ultimate Battle by Bill Sloan. I refer you to those references to learn more about the intricacies of the Battle for Okinawa, what turned out to be the final land battle of World War II. The invasion began on April 1 and lasted about 82 days. When it was over 150,000 Okinawans (one third of the island's native population), 90,000 Japanese, and 12,000 Americans were dead. There was not one Okinawan family that was not affected by loss. The Navy suffered its worst fatalities in the war, approximately 5500 dead and thousands wounded, most by kamikaze and the remainder as Navy Corpsmen in battle assisting wounded Marines.

L-Day, as it was called on Okinawa, was unlike most landings; relatively quiet with minimal casualties. The 6th Marine Division headed straight across the midsection of the island, turned left and headed north. Over the next 4 to 5 weeks they secured 50% of the island. The First Marine

Division and some Army units headed east and south. At the time they did not realize, but they were heading into the major defensive line of the Japanese Army. The Japanese, as on Iwo Jima, developed an intricate system of tunnels and supply lines throughout all the hills to supply and re-supply the front line. Resistance increased against the U.S. forces as they headed south. One of the tactical problems in managing those battles was having Army and Marines flanking each other. Marine strategy in battle differed from Army (at least it did in World War II). Marines moved forward at a faster pace than the Army did. They ran to the enemy. The end result was to become outflanked. The enemy was now found between the slower Army and the faster advancing Marines. This situation, which had already occurred in Saipan, placed the Marines and Army in vulnerable positions of crossfire from the enemy.

Well-documented in many books are the behind-the-scenes arguments that ensued between top brass over this dilemma. It is not my intent to shed a bad light on the Army. Their tactics were different from the Marines and did not mesh well, side by side. The end result was generally the same. Marines and Army would suffer similar fatalities and casualties. The Marines would simply reach their stated objective sooner.

A problem was breaking out on this front which came to be known as the Shuri Line. This was a large corral ridge that bisected the central island. On the top and center of this range stood Shuri Castle where the Japanese commanders dug in to defend the island. A National Guard unit, the 27th Division from New York, was holed up on the Shuri Line being hammered and for whatever reason refused or could not advance. The battle to the south was at a standstill. According to George Feifer's book, Admiral Nimitz flew to Okinawa to have some "straight talk with General (Buckner) over the situation."9 The battle had to move forward as the Navy was being pummeled by the kamikaze.   Because of the close proximity to mainland Japan, hundreds of Japanese were sent out in Zeroes with just enough fuel for a one-way suicide mission. The worst kamikaze attacks of World War II occurred off the west coast of Okinawa, where more Navy ships sat than on D-Day Normandy.

The commanding generals made the decision to switch the 27th Army Division with the 6th Marine Division. So in late April, the Marines marched south on "Highway 1" and on the other side of the road, the stunned 27th Army marched north. Lt. Jamieson spent most of his day breaking up fights between cocky advancing Marines and the bewildered retreating soldiers. Here are Roger's recollections of his time in Okinawa. He wrote these memoirs on November 15, 1994, but it is evident to me that the memory was as clear as if it happened yesterday. Italicized remarks are mine.

"Our landing at Okinawa occurred on 1 April 1945, which was both Easter Sunday and April Fools' Day, probably signaling some kind of irony. *(All Marines had been given a steak and eggs breakfast at 3AM and many of the men had hurled it on board the landing vehicles while circling for hours before landing)* This time I was on the sixth wave but there was none of the excitement experienced at Guam. There were just a few casualties in the whole 6th Mardiv the first day; we turned North, which was our primary assignment and by April 22 we had secured the northern end of the island without suffering heavy casualties. The only thing I experienced up till now was a bad case of fleas, which afflicted many others and, when we finally got some flea powder, we were able to disinfect our clothes. We stayed up North until early May at which time we swapped places with the Army 27th, which had been doing nothing down South. Down South, with us (the 6th Mardiv, that is) there with the 1st Mardiv, an offensive was started, which was rough and therefore costly; the days of light casualties were over. My job in coding included travel by jeep from 6th Mardiv. Hq. mainly to the three regimental headquarters; I would see one after the other of jeep ambulances carrying Marine bodies back from the front; they were deposited on racks with the feet sticking out of the back, bouncing up and down. After many days of seeing this I simply decided I didn't like my comparatively safe duty any more and that I wanted to do more. On May 13 I came back from my messenger run, went to my tent, lay on my cot, and thought about it. After about ten minutes I went to see Major Overstreet and told him I wanted line duty. He argued with me and cussed me out a bit, but I told him if I weren't transferred I'd go anyway. This made him really mad but we kept talking and he finally agreed to a transfer. The main issue here really was that those not at the front usually didn't like to be made to feel that they weren't really contributing; when a buck like me came along yelling any suggestion like that, it was something that today would be considered politically incorrect.

I was taken to the 22nd Marine Regiment, sent to 2nd Battalion, assigned to F company, and was given 25 buck privates and a second lieutenant. I was told to disperse them in a designated area, have them all dig in, be ready to move out in the morning. Before dark we were all dug in. This was the first foxhole and the first night of combat for the 25 and the first night of combat for my 2nd Lt. Though I knew things were rough out there, and I knew we'd be there soon, it didn't occur to me that it could be (and it became) the last night of combat for all of them. These kids were at this point in the Marine Corps for 8 weeks. The 2nd Lt. said he was in 6 months; two-thirds of that would have been Officer Training at Quantico, Virginia. I had no possible chance to learn much about them, not even their names, but I talked to them at length, in effect told them to look to me for instructions wherever we were; I had no sergeant, no corporal. We got into our foxholes and didn't get to sleep.

At about 2130 hours (9:30 p.m.) a runner came up and said the company commander wanted to see me right away. I don't remember the company commander's name or rank [normally a company commander was a captain but, if one is removed (killed, wounded, relieved) during combat, it could be a lieutenant or a noncommissioned officer], but Lt. Col. Woodhouse, the battalion Commanding Officer, was there with him. Woodhouse and I knew each other, and he asked me the status of my troops. I told him they were all just straight out of boot camp except the 2nd Lt., who was just out of OCS. He said, "I hate to have to do this, but I'm sending you right now up to our front; we're at a place called Sugar Loaf Hill. A tractor will be here soon; put your men on it and report to my executive officer, Major Courtney, when you get there." I never saw or heard Woodhouse again, and he was later killed.

My recollection is that we reached the Sugar Loaf at about 2230; we unloaded the tractor near the base of the hill (mainly crates of hand grenades and .30 caliber ammunition), where Courtney told my men to spread out and hit the deck. He took me and the 2nd Lt. over to where a couple of other guys were, one of whom was 1st Lt. Pesely. It was determined that Pesely was senior to me and was nominally second in command. Courtney explained to all of us that he wanted to take the hill since he felt our position at the base of it would be worse than if we were on the hill, that the Japs would have the high ground and we would be exposed especially after sunup. He wanted us to get the grenades and ammo part way up the hill first so that it would be more accessible than having to go down to the bottom when it was needed; also, if the Japs pulled a flanker and overran our supplies, we would be in serious trouble. So we all dropped our weapons (mine was a carbine, a light .30 caliber rifle, smaller and much less reliable than the standard M1 carried by the enlisted men) and spent maybe a half-hour each lugging two crates at a time up the hill about 15 or 20 yards. When this was done, he ordered everybody to spread out around the base of the hill, standing; he yelled, "Let's take the damn hill!" He stepped forward, and I will never forget how all the rest of us, all together as if a whistle had blown to signal the start of a game, stepped out after him. Including me and my 26, there were about 50 of us.

We proceeded on foot about halfway up the hill where Courtney yelled, "Hit the deck!" The Japs were at the crest of the hill throwing grenades at us; we had all picked up as many grenades as we could carry, and we retaliated as we crept up the hill. The Japs disappeared from the crest; at this point we had the hill and we were winning. There were some Japs on the forward slope because we were catching some grenades from there.

Then, several things happened in fairly rapid order; one of my kids, next to me at my left, fumbled a grenade after he had pulled the pin, and my nose dug a hole in the ground. The grenade exploded and apparently hit nobody. I got up, went over to the kid, gave him a kick on the rump with the side of my right foot and then gave him a quick lesson in hand grenade - how to hold it, how to pull the pin, how long to hold it after pulling the pin, how to throw it, together with a personal demonstration. Then I ordered him to throw one, which he did, and he did alright. Although I had earlier (back at the company command post before we sacked in) emphatically instructed everybody to call me "Jamieson" and not "Lieutenant", this liability on my left said, "Thanks, Lieutenant," to which I replied, "Shut up!" Although my actions in this scenario were called for under the circumstances (again, today they would be called politically incorrect), I have never felt good about them considering I did make it off the hill alive and this poor kid died with my kick and my reply probably the last communication he had with anybody.

At the time, though, I didn't dwell on it. Moments later a shell (most likely a mortar) dropped to my right, and it hit the kid on my right. He started screaming and I crept over to him; he apparently had been hit in the area of the left shoulder. I yelled for a corpsman (we went up the hill with two), but he didn't show. So I stood up, picked up the kid in a fireman's carry with him yelling, "Don't, Lieutenant, you'll get killed," and me issuing my second "Shut up" of the night. I shifted him on my left shoulder before I started downhill with him and, as I did, I saw Courtney go down; at the time it looked as though he had tripped or slipped. Later, I learned that he had been hit and killed.

I carried my kid downhill to what was more or less a ledge, laid him down, and a corpsman nearby came over. He bandaged him, gave me a couple of bandages to finish the job, and took off to answer other calls. He and the other corpsman were killed during the night. I was just finishing tying up my kid when something hit us. I had been lying on my right arm with the kid's legs and body underneath it while tying the bandage strings. This blast picked me up and my face hit the ground about where my feet had been. The kid was screaming and bleeding very badly; this shell must have hit between him and the coral wall we were laying next to, and he caught most of it. Some other wounded, lying nearby but apparently not hit by this one, threw me a few bandages, but they were not adequate for the bleeding he was doing. I looked for his dog tags and couldn't find them. I asked him to quiet down and listen to me. I asked him about the dog tags; he said they didn't issue any. So I asked him for his name and home address, which I wrote down and placed inside his helmet. He was yelling about his mother, and I told him I was going to see about a tractor coming up so he could be taken back to a field hospital where he'd be all right. (He died that night.)

I found Pesely on the other side of the hill, near where we had started up the hill; he was behind our radio in a sort of individual dugout. I told him I had a badly wounded kid and asked if there would be any tractors coming up. He said there would be nothing until the morning. He also told me Courtney was dead. At this point, I realized my right arm was bleeding and I could hardly move it. So I bandaged it. Pesely told me to spread the men along the reverse slope and also send some around the right side of the hill to protect that flank. I found my 2nd Lt., gave him five or six men, and assigned him to the right flank with orders to hold. It was pushing 0200.

The rest of the night was a constant round of first quiet, then enemy bombardment, then flares shot up from our ships in the bay when the bombardment stopped; usually the flares showed Japs running toward us and running back when our machine gun fire and other fire [BAR's (Browning Automatic Rifles), for example] started to hit them. Then, quiet again. Etc. There was rain, but I don't remember being wet or cold. Does adrenaline take care of those also? (*Roger also mentioned to me how close they were to the enemy. They could see them and hear them talking. At one point, they heard the Japanese soldiers yell "F*** Roosevelt", or" F*** Babe Ruth" as if such insults would dishearten the Marines and then they would lob off some grenades. The Marines would reply with "F*** Tojo" in response and lob some grenades back. This surreal atmosphere added a touch of humor to an otherwise intense struggle.*)

About 0330 one of our guys at or near the top of the hill yelled, "Here they come - there must a hundred of them." At first I thought he meant another attack, but instead behind us came what turned out to be about 35 more Marines on foot, and they came up the hill as cocky as can be and as though they were going to show us how it should be done. One machine gun squad set up right near the foxhole I was in at the time, was about ready to commence firing when a shell hit and wiped out the whole team. The bombardment stopped, the flares went up, the Japs came running, our guys sent them running back (that is, some of them who were lucky; I don't know how many of them were killed that night), then quiet again. Several times I went to Pesely who was on the radio with Woodhouse all night so that, for one thing, when bombardment stopped he could ask for the flares. I did this in case any change in approach occurred to him or headquarters.

At about 0550 I heard a yell, which was probably Pesely, ordering everybody off; a tractor had come up; I looked down the hill, saw a few guys running toward it, so I got up and headed for it also. I got on, the ramp went up a couple of minutes later, and the tractor pulled out. There were 9 of us, all wounded - no more, no less.

We were transported to an aid station where there were some doctors in attendance. We were examined from the standpoint of being taken care of locally or being flown to Guam where our division rear echelon was setting up camp as our next (after Okinawa) forward training base. I was examined by a Dr. Jamieson from Buffalo, New York; he and I had gotten to know each other being aboard the same transport ship en route to Okinawa. He put me on the plane to Guam, which left on 16 May. It was a C-54, a four-engine transport, the largest we had then, and it was a workhorse for most of the war. On the plane there were a couple of Army nurses, who spent most of their time talking and tending to the most seriously wounded; the rest of us didn't really mind; in fact, we knew it should be that way, and we all didn't apparently feel like talking to each other and the flight (though it was my first) became boring.

On Guam we were put into a Navy hospital and on the second day I had a ruckus with one of the doctors, a lieutenant commander, who criticized the fact that I had been flown since my wound wasn't much. I told him he could blow it out his ass and said that I didn't buy the ticket. Also, my arm was still stiff and it hurt and what about that? He did nothing and two days later I was released and sent to what was called the Casualty Battalion to await further assignment. Two days later, my arm swelled and hurt more; I was sent back to the hospital for exam and the same doc became my doc or tried to. I told him I didn't want his opinion and we started cussing each other out, which caused another doctor, a captain, to come out to see what was going on. The first doc said I was being troublesome and the captain asked me what was my problem. I pointed to the first doc and said, "He is the problem." I then explained the exchanges I had had with the first doc, that I had no confidence in him, just wanted to see what was wrong with my arm. The captain took over, guessed the arm was infected, figured some shrapnel might still be in it, stuck a needle in the arm, probed around, pulled out about a half-inch piece of metal. He treated and bandaged it, and I went back to Casualty Battalion. On 31 May I was told I had the choice of going to the 6th Mardiv rear echelon on Guam or going back to Okinawa. I chose Okinawa and shipped out on 10 June on the S.S. Fairland, a Merchant Marine ship. We reached Okinawa on 16 June.

On 17 June, at 6th Mardiv Hq., I was sent to good ol' Major Overstreet. Also there was Lt. Col. Elby D. Martin, Jr. (Division Communications Officer), who told me I didn't have to go back to the front with the 22nd, that he could put me back in communications. But I told him I wanted to go back to the 22nd, that they must still need officers there. He said, "You really want it, don't you?" I said yes.

At this time, I was in khaki with no equipment. I was able to get a helmet and was told I could get a weapon and dungarees at a supply dump near the front. A jeep pulling a little trailer was pulling out with four guys in the jeep. I hitched a ride on the trailer, and we headed toward 2nd Battalion, the 22nd. We passed one spot on a dirt road where we all had to duck sniper fire and shortly after we had to stop because a big boulder was in the middle of the road. As we were all getting out to see if we could move the boulder out of our way, something (probably a knee mortar) hit us, actually, four of us. The biggest guy, who was about 6'3 and 200-plus, was unwounded, and he was the only one who left the jeep with a weapon. Two guys were slightly wounded, I had just a little stinger on the top of my left shoulder, but one guy was hit on the right forearm and was bleeding badly. I asked the big guy if he would try to get back to a field first aid station we had passed on the road; this was about a half-mile back. He shook his head no. I said O.K. and lend me your rifle and I'll go, but he wouldn't do that either.

We had all jumped into a ditch on the right-hand side of the road since we all apparently figured the shot had come from the left. I don't know why we figured that but I soon found out we were wrong. I started to creep and crawl, maybe went about twenty yards when something hit again. As best I could tell another shell had missed me but hit the side of the ditch and a mess of metal and coral plastered me in the right shoulder blade area and flattened me to the ground. I then heard some heavy feet, looked up, and here comes the guy with the bad arm running like all get out. A shot whistled past us, and it didn't take a great decision for me to get up and follow the other guy. We both reached the aid station where the corpsmen tore our shirts off, gave us each two syrettes of morphine, and treated the wounds. While this was being done I told them about the other two wounded and the one unwounded and a couple of corpsmen and two Marines went out. The two Marines flushed out the sniper and the corpsmen were able to treat the two wounded on the spot, I don't know what happened to the unwounded guy. This probably was during the battle at Mezado Ridge. I was put on a tractor, was taken to Division Hq., where I had a brief visit with my old pals in Coding (one of them broke out a bottle of bourbon much of which I swallowed, which wasn't smart at all on top of the morphine but I wasn't exactly putting two and two together).

That night I was on a cot in a bunker protected above by a pile of sandbags along with many other wounded. I didn't sleep all night, chain-smoked cigarettes all night long, which I guess was the result of the morphine/bourbon combination plus my own adrenaline. The next day, 18 June,

I was put on a hospital ship, the U.S.S. Rescue, and we left for Guam the next day. We reached Guam on 23 June and I was put in a Navy Hospital, Base 18, where I found the second lieutenant who was with me at Sugar Loaf - the tenth man.

He told me that he had heard the orders to leave the hill but he couldn't get up. He heard the tractor pull out, and he said a few minutes later the Japs were running all over the place. He was lying face down in a ditch and lay still attempting to pretend he was dead, which worked. When all the Jap noise subsided and he thought maybe they weren't close by, he started to crawl or drag himself (he was severely wounded in the left shoulder area), would stop if he heard anything, and after several hours he crawled into the 2nd Battalion forward command post. They asked him where he had come from. He told them Sugar Loaf, and they said that that was three miles away. He asked me what had happened to me, and I filled him in. I wish I could remember his name."

The Marines would capture and lose the hill several times over the ensuing week. It would take the Sixth Marine Division another six days to finally run the Japanese off Sugar Hill for good.

Lt. Jamieson, September 1945, soon after his return from Okinawa

Betty Alexander, with a four leaf clover she found. Roger carried this laminated photo with him at all times during his Pacific tour.

"You have an inferiority complex and you try to cover it up by acting as though you have a superiority complex."
Betty Alexander, circa 1936, response to Roger Jamieson's antics in class at East Side High

"When I came home from Okinawa by ship in 1945, I was speechless when I saw the Golden Gate Bridge appear on the horizon."
Roger Jamieson, July 27, 1995

CHAPTER 6

Coming Home

I had mentioned in an earlier chapter that Roger was friends and academic rivals with Betty Alexander. They sparred for grades in college prep classes for four years. At one point, Betty, exasperated by Roger's playful but argumentative spirit, quipped the above-mentioned quote in class. This particular quote left Roger speechless (a rarity), and he never forgot what Betty had said to him.

Both graduated with honors out of East Side High School and went on to college. Betty attended Elmira College in Elmira, New York, and studied nursing. As mentioned previously, Roger went on to Muhlenberg College in Allentown, Pennsylvania. Since each traveled in different social circles, neither saw each other for six years. Some time in October of 1943, after Roger had successfully completed officers' training school and before heading down to Camp LeJeune for "permanent duty beyond the seas," Roger was given a 10-day leave. He came home to Paterson, New Jersey to see his family and friends before shipping off. He decided to pay a visit on his first Saturday night to one William E. Alexander, former shop and mechanical drafting teacher at East Side High. Roger was known to Mr. Alexander, not only from East Side High, but the Jamiesons were well known in the city of Paterson, especially because of Charlie Jamieson, the baseball player. Bill Alexander would come and watch Roger play for the Chevrolet Red Sox. So Roger showed up and sat down and talked. William Alexander was a strict, disciplined, no-nonsense, Irish Catholic, take-no-prisoners kind of guy; a proud man, 6 foot tall, a superb athlete and educator. The conversation eventually turned to his daughter, Betty. Roger had asked, "How's Betty?" Bill answered, "She is working in a hospital in New York City. In fact, she is due home any minute for a visit." My cousin, Bill Ganon, suspecting ulterior motives said later of that meeting, "Roger is home on leave for 10 days from the Marines and the first stop on his leave on a Saturday night is to visit William and Elizabeth Alexander and to see how they are doing. Now, for those who don't know William Alexander, first, he was an Irishman, secondly he was a tough Irishman, the son of a police detective in Paterson. He was very competitive. He was an ex-wrestler, football player and swimmer, with numerous awards. He was extraordinarily precise. He ran a strict classroom at East Side High; not the kind of guy you stop in on your first day of leave from the Marines to see how Bill's doing...He's doing fine, Rog, what's the next question?" Although Roger denies any ulterior motive, he off-handedly throws out the comment, "By the way, how's Betty?" As providence would have it, Betty just happens to show up in her fur coat and stylish hat and as Roger later admitted, "Va-va-va-voom; sparks flew."

The next 10 days, Roger and Betty dated. Roger would meet Betty in New York City and they would go out to one of the many famous ballrooms to listen to the likes of Tommy Dorsey, Benny Goodman, Hal Kemp, Kay Keyser and Harry James. They danced the nights away to tunes like "All the Things You Are", "Smoke Rings", and "I'll Never Smile Again". By the final evening, Roger proposed and Betty accepted; no money, no ring, unknown future— just a promise after a whirlwind courtship. I asked her later about a 10-day dating spree that ended up in an engagement. How could that happen? They were respected friends in high school, but nothing romantic. Six years of separation and out of the blue Roger shows up and 10 days later, they're engaged? She put it this way; "The war compressed time. You had to live for the now. Young men were going overseas and being killed or maimed. Leaves were short."

Roger never confided with me as to what he was thinking about before the night he paid a visit to Bill and Liz Alexander, but my guess is he knew he would be shipping out to points unknown in the vast Pacific. He probably thought about Betty Alexander and decided to go for it; to have someone back home to fight for and to care for. But Roger was not out-wardly romantic, so he never admitted to me his thinking here. But he left for Camp LeJeune and Rex Dillow remembers soon after they met that Roger did have a girlfriend, about whom he was very serious and to whom he would write every day. He often had to finish his daily letters in the restroom, the only place with lights after taps. And Roger did confide that he wrote Betty every day he was not in combat. When he had enough money, he mailed it to her so that she could buy a ring.

Fast-forward from October 1943 to July 1945. After Roger's second wound, he was transferred to the rear echelon of the 22nd Marines in Guam, where he recovered. He was then returned to the United States in accor-dance with Marine Corps policy for twice-wounded Marines. Roger initially argued with his commanding officer that he wanted to go back to Okinawa, but his request was denied. So in mid-July, he embarked aboard the USS Long Island and sailed to Hawaii. They were given two days of leave there. He and a fellow officer had a bit too much to drink and fell asleep on the beaches of Waikiki. On July 29, he departed on the same ship for San Francisco. My father was the highest-ranking Marine officer on the ship. The cruiser transported approximately 20 Marines coming home from months of battle. It was a rowdy group to contain. A lot of drinking, cards, and antics went on each evening. Each morning, Roger had to report to the bridge to explain the Marines' escapades from the night before. There was really nothing Roger could do or explain away and the Navy brass sort of understood that the Marines had to decompress and let off steam. After 14 riotous days and nights at sea from Guam, it was announced on August 4 in the morning that the U.S. mainland was in sight. Roger recalled all the Marines stood on deck silently as they passed under the Golden Gate Bridge; not a peep or a word. Roger got choked up telling me the story. They never thought they would see home again; now here they were. They made it! One of the reasons I believe Roger came to love San Francisco and the Golden Gate Bridge was the nostalgia of that moment. The bridge and the city represented home and safety. (In the summer of 1993, Roger got the entire family together for a family reunion in San Francisco. The extended family stayed at the Marine Corps Memorial Hotel and Roger arranged for a family photograph from the Marin Headlands, overlooking the Bay and the Golden Gate Bridge.) Roger reported to headquarters Department of the Pacific Marine Corps at 100 Hansen Street, San Francisco and was given six weeks rehab/leave. Roger found a hotel, grabbed a bite, and called Betty, now a commissioned Navy officer and nurse who was stationed at Rhode Island Naval Station. Four days by railroad found Roger in Providence on August 11, 1945. They decided that day to see about getting a marriage license. They went to the county clerk's office which was located on the second floor of a bank. A bank clerk, Bob Annon, sat them down and said he knew a place about 10 miles away, and he began making phone calls. They had only planned to get a license that day, not get married. This kind clerk, however, when he got off the phone, said he had a church and a minister. Bob and his wife, Peg would be the witnesses. Betty and Roger looked at each other, shrugged, and said why not? They were married in a lovely old Congregational Church in Pawtucket, Rhode Island at Park Place Congregational. The minister was a bit apprehensive at first, thinking that this was just a fly-by-night thing, but when he discovered that Roger and Betty had gone to high school together and knew each other well, he was very happy and performed a lovely service. They had their honeymoon at the Biltmore Hotel in Providence, Rhode Island, staying on the fifth floor. When they called their folks in New Jersey, all were very upset. Betty was Catholic and Roger was Protestant, but more than that, the parents all just felt left out. Three days after they were married, up in their hotel room at 5:00 a.m., they heard loud booms and shooting noises. Roger responded by diving under the bed, still under the influence of the effects of war. Betty grabbed his legs as he dove, wondering what was going on. They crawled over to the window and looked out. There were crowds of people, firecrackers, and shouting. "What's going on?" they shouted down to the crowds. "The Japs have surrendered!!" was the joyous reply. The next day, Roger sent telegrams to both parents saying, "The war's over; let's end ours." They went to New Jersey next to see their folks. They came up in a taxi to a hotel in town and went to the receptionist. The receptionist dusted them off and stated there were no rooms. A gentleman, however, out front (who later became mayor of Paterson) said, "Hey, soldier, what do you want?" Roger responded, "I'm not a soldier" (he was a Marine). "You and your girl want a room?" the man asked. "This isn't my girl, this is my wife," Roger answered. "OK," the man said, "whatever; wait here." He went in and when he came out, he had the keys to a room for Roger and Betty. They called their folks, who both wanted to come and get them. They decided that Roger's parents should pick them up. They hadn't seen their son since he'd been home. They went to the Jamieson's home and were greeted warmly. Dad's Uncle David and Aunt Agnes Dougherty were there waiting all day for Roger's return and said, "We're proud of you, Rog. We only wish you could have brought David home with you." Aunt Aggie meant no harm by this statement, but Roger broke when he told me this story and really cried. It hurt then and it still did.

Next they went to Betty's folks'. Bill, her father, sat them down and said seriously, "Tell me, was this necessary?" implying Betty might be pregnant. Betty said, "Dad, Roger has been away for one and a half years and home for two days. How could it be necessary?" At this point, he relaxed and said, "Congratulations" and handed his new son-in-law $500.00, a lot of money back then. Betty resigned from the Navy and Roger, after recovering from a case of hepatitis A, was assigned to Lake Denmark Naval Station in New Jersey. There he finished out his four-year active duty career with the U.S. Marine Corps.

PART II:

1995
Return to Okinawa

"Notice the calm cool efficiency with which I work."

Roger Jamieson, ca. 1970s

Chapter 7

The Year of Preparation

Soon after getting a commitment with Dad to go, I had to find out if there would, in fact, be a 50th anniversary commemorative tour in Okinawa. I first called the Marine Corps Memorial Club. The staff referred me on to the Marine Corps Association in Quantico, Virginia. There I learned that there would be a tour and I was referred to Military Historical Tours. This company specialized in World War II, Korea, and Vietnam tours for veterans.

I called and they sent me information. It turned out that they were currently up to their necks working on the 50th Saipan and Guam tours (1944 to 1994), and would start work on Okinawa after the 1994 tours were complete.

I began reading anything I could get my hands on about Okinawa. I went to the local library and checked out several books. The first few books, like <u>Okinawa</u> by Frank Benis, read like history books, but it gave me a great overview of the battles, the strategy, and the leadership personalities. It showed where the First Marine Division and Sixth Marine Division and the Army went. I learned about the kamikaze raids and the toll on the U.S. Navy. I read about Sugar Loaf Hill with interest.

I couldn't tell you how many calls I made to Dad that summer as I read different accounts of the Battle for Okinawa. I would compare his recollections with the books I read — many had conflicting facts. I was never in the military so I did not always understand the lingo or the logistics. Dad knew it all and could explain precisely what the history books were saying and also correct what was in error. Something I came to realize is that everybody had a different memory or a different perspective just like eyewitness accounts of a single accident.

On one of my visits to the library, I stumbled upon a different type of book about Okinawa. The book was called <u>Tennozan,</u> (that's a Japanese word meaning decisive struggle), <u>The Battle for Okinawa and the Atomic Bomb</u> by George Feifer. This was a 584-page volume of research published in 1992. I believe it was a work that took the author 10 years to produce. The beauty of this masterpiece for me revolved around how Feifer followed a Japanese officer, a conscripted Okinawan boy, Mashide Ota, and several 6th Marine Division Marines during the three-month battle. All the history was there, but the personalized testimony from all sides made this book a captivating read. I corresponded with the author on several occasions. It turned out he got his inspiration for the book while chopping wood with his neighbor, Dick Whitaker, a 6th Marine Division Okinawa veteran. Dick opened up to George, which started the wheels turning.

This book includes a very thorough account of the Battle for Sugar Loaf Hill. Dad got a copy and began reading. He recognized a few names in the book from the night Dad had fought on Sugar Loaf Hill and Major Courtney was killed. Lieutenant Ed Pesely then became first in command and my dad became second in command. Dad was as captivated by this book as I was.

When I felt I had read enough about Okinawa, my thoughts turned to Dad's cousin, David Leslie Dougherty. All I knew at this point is that Dad had a cousin, David who was killed fighting somewhere in the Pacific.

I called my dad one day and asked him on what island did David die? Dad paused a bit, and quietly said, "Saipan." I got out a map, located Saipan. It is located just 60 miles north of Guam in the Marianas Island chain. I began reading about the battle and then Guam. Again, I made several back-and-forth calls to Dad, asking questions, having discussions, and getting answers and understanding.

It began to dawn on me that if we were going to travel all the way to Okinawa, why not stop in and visit Guam and Saipan? We had not as yet made final preparations with the company, as it was only late summer — 10 months before the 50th anniversary commemorative tour. After several letters and calls to Military Historic Tours, I found out that we could arrange our own transportation to and from Okinawa and pay for a "land-only" tour package. It turned out that Continental and its international flight subsidiary, Continental Micronesia, flew out of San Francisco to Hawaii to Guam to Okinawa and Saipan, so I reserved two seats with my dad's blessing. The entire trip would last 14 days with approximately one week on Okinawa, a day on Guam, a day on Saipan, plus two days in Hawaii and the travel time.

At the time of the reservation, we weren't sure what we would do on Guam or Saipan, but we had 10 months to figure that out.

In the late summer, I talked to one of my patients, Tara Magofna, who lived and taught school in Saipan and vacationed in Keizer, Oregon, in the summer. She told me that there was a war memorial erected there this last summer for the 50th anniversary celebration that had been held. I asked her, upon her return, to find out if David Leslie Dougherty's name was on the monument. A month or so later, I received several pictures of the landing beaches, the war memorial, and a close-up picture of the monument with David Leslie Dougherty's name. I sent that off to Dad. This information from Tara added increased impetus for us to visit Saipan.

Fall 1994 kept me reading books on every Marine landing from Guadalcanal, Bougainville, Tarawa, the Marshalls, the Marianas, Peleliu to Iwo Jima.

I also became more and more obsessed and preoccupied with David Leslie Dougherty and my dad. Several strong feelings were welling up inside me. I couldn't quite put my finger on what was going on. I had never met David Leslie Dougherty. I had, on several occasions, met my elderly Great Aunt Agnes, whom we called Aunt Aggie, and my Great Uncle Dave, his parents, when they would visit our house in New Jersey for an after-church Sunday meal. My Uncle David Dougherty had a profound kyphosis or hunchback. He was gregarious and vociferous. My Great Aunt Aggie was a bit more reserved.

I know my dad harbored deep-seated feelings of sadness about David. He felt personally responsible for his cousin's death because David Leslie Dougherty joined the Marines because Dad had. Dad also felt a certain guilt surviving his ordeal, coming home and raising a family. David Leslie Dougherty was the Dougherty's only child. Dad named his first son after David L. As my dad stated later in 1995 during a Stars and Stripes inter-view, " We were as thick as brothers….It's something you carry with you the rest of your life and nobody can tell you how to drop it."[10] The more I read that autumn and the more I talked with Dad on the phone, the more he would open up.

Some ideas were forming in my head about my dad and about David and the close brotherly relationship they had forged as children and young men. David was killed on D-Day, June 15, 1944, while attempting to land at Saipan. Dad and David had last been together when both were stationed in Honolulu. David was at the naval hospital recovering from dysentery he contracted while fighting in the Marshalls (Roi Namur). The rest of his squad were training and regrouping at Camp Maui located in the upcoun-try of North Maui.

Somehow David found out that Dad was training in Honolulu and he located him. David didn't even have a uniform, but Dad found one and they took one and went on liberty. While walking down Kalakaua Avenue on Waikiki in front of the Moana Hotel, a photographer snapped a photo and asked if they wanted a copy to send back to the States for their parents. Dad initially dusted the pushy hawker off, and David and Dad walked away. David stopped and suggested the folks back home might like a photo and at 25 cents, it was a fair deal. It is the only photo I have found of the two. Though they couldn't know it then, it would be the last recording of the two together.

These vignettes and many other stories Dad told me began churning in my mind. How could I express the emotions I was feeling? I felt sorry for David, taken out of this world at 19 years old; the loss to his many cousins, his parents, numerous aunts and uncles and friends. Letters we have received after our trip revealed David was quite athletic, a friend to all, and a favorite amongst the young ladies. In the prime of his life, he sacrificed his life for our freedom, and Dad now 50 years after David Leslie Dougherty's death, was still hurting inside, blaming himself. One rainy November Sunday in 1994, our family went off to church, which is our usual custom. We attend a large, non-denominational church called Morning Star Community Church. The first 30 minutes of church service is spent singing choruses. It is a time in the service to worship God in praise. Sometimes it can be an emotional experience. That Sunday as we all began singing, a sentence or two came to my mind about Dad and David Leslie Dougherty, then another line, and another. I grabbed the Sunday service bulletin and with a pen began to write. With tears in my eyes and a thousand people singing praise hymns, I wrote down what came into my head. The poem I wrote, came about in 10 to 15 minutes in pieces, not in order; first the second or third verse, then the first, then the last verse. I feel that the poem, Two Men, was a gift inspired by God that very concisely expressed those many feelings that had been pent up inside me for several months. What a catharsis! I showed the poem to my wife, written in its final order. I believe I only changed one word of it from the original revelation. I tucked it away and decided I would present the poem to Dad at a proper time, later.

Sgt.Grant's Squad: Clockwise from upper left; Pierre LaLancette,
John Carter, Harold Mentzel, Leo Kelly, David Dougherty, Bill Hewitt,
Richard Simpkins Sgt. Grant, Arthur Yancy, Charles Wolf,
James "Sammy" Sampson and John Dewine. Not Pictured: Jack Jones

"We gave our all to be #1. That's quite a goal, but we were all on the same page...and we worked hard to be the first no matter what the challenge."
Sgt. Jack Grant, Squad leader, 2nd Squad, 3rd Platoon, C-1-25, 4th Marine Division

CHAPTER 8

Finding PFC Dougherty's Squad

By now, I had learned many things about Okinawa and the entire Pacific Theater. I had read a lot about Saipan. We were about 2 and a half months away from our trip to Okinawa, Guam, and Saipan, and I began dwelling on the idea of finding any survivors who knew David Dougherty. I felt it was an essential piece of the puzzle for my father to resolve some of his war wounds. As mentioned earlier, Dad said that he had first heard of David's probable death when on Guam, when Grandpa Jamieson wrote him. He wrote saying that David was listed as missing in action.

It was later confirmed that David was killed in action. Dad heard about this while he was training in Guadalcanal. As Rex Dillow recalled Dad was despondent for several days. From this point the war became very personal to Dad. Without David's body returned, back in Paterson, on Sunday, September 30, 1945 the Church of the Messiah held a memorial service. The program read "Our Tribute of Honor to P.F.C. David L Dougherty, reported killed in action on Saipan, June 15 1944." There was some ambiguity in the program when it said "reported killed in action." And I remember once my father telling me that Aunt Aggie never relinquished hope that the report was a terrible mix up and David someday would show up at her front door. Cousin Donald Jamieson, then a teenager, was an eyewitness to these events as they unfurled in Paterson. He said, "The worst visit I ever had to Aggie's and Dave's was when they received word that David was missing in action. The whole family was there and it was a terrible experience for everyone. There was never closure until his body was returned…" And Cousin John Jamieson added, "Aunt Aggie and Uncle Dave were never the same after their loss."

But what really happened there on Saipan? Was there anyone alive 51 years later who could tell us? My dad somehow had information that David was one of 17 in his platoon who were killed landing on Saipan. David's remains were shipped back from Saipan to Hawthorne, N.J. in 1949 and buried there. My dad had his doubts that the remains shipped were really those of his cousin. He never shared his thoughts with David's parents or anyone until recently.

I had a gut feeling there must be someone out there who knew more information. It had not been too difficult to locate three of Dad's comrades. I had found Ed Pesely thanks to George Feifer. He got me in contact with Dick Whitaker who had his phone number. I gave the number to Dad when he was visiting me and he called Mr. Pesley. They had a 45 minute talk. I found Rex Dillow thanks to a lead from Dad. He had not seen Rex since Guadalcanal. He remembered he grew up in Carbondale, Illinois. I had friends, Andy and Michelle Wist in nearby Murphysboro, Illinois and I asked them to look up any Dillows in the phonebook. Without explanation, I received a letter from Michelle with Rex Dillow's name and address in Missouri. Dad called him and later visited his old WWII buddy. I had found an address for Buck Osborne. He had gotten his law degree and was a partner in a large law firm in Florida. Sadly, he had passed away, but Dad and Mom later got to visit his widow and had a nice time reminiscing. Now, I needed to find a connection with David Leslie Dougherty.

I knew that David was in Company C First Battalion 25th Regiment of the 4th Marine Division. On April 3, 1995, I sent a letter to John Stone, executive secretary and editor for the 4th Marine Division Association newsletter, asking for help.

I believe it was John who gave me the name of Joseph Berry in nearby Gresham, Oregon, who had a "red book" — a picture book from World War II of all of the 25th Regiment. Mr. Berry sent me a photocopy of all the Marines in Company C. I had narrowed the list down to 200.

I then wrote Mr. Stone and asked for an address list. Mind you, all of this research was done without the use of the internet (because in 1994, Al Gore was still inventing it). He wrote down 15 names, C through K on his list. Note that Mr. Stone did all of this by hand, cross-referencing 4th Marine Division Association members with C-1-25. This was a labor-intensive and time consuming task. Mr. Stone said to try these first 15 and if no success, he would send me more names. I sent out a form letter explaining about David, pictures from the yearbook, and maps of the assault of Saipan. I sent the letter out in early May 1995.

By now, I was in the thick of coaching Joseph, my son, in Little League. If not coaching, I was watching Dave and Dan in Babe Ruth League, or Holly in soccer. I would receive a few short notes back from men on the list. Typically the letter would sound like this: "Hadn't heard of him." "Good luck." "I joined after Saipan and went to Iwo." I received a few phone calls from lonely Marine vets in VA nursing homes back East. I would listen to them tell their stories, I would finally ask them if they knew David Dougherty, and the answer was no. I always thanked them for their service to our country. I felt these poor men were so lonely they called just to have someone to talk to. I began to realize the hope of finding anyone was a needle in a haystack.

One early May evening, I came home at 8:30 p.m. from coaching a game and there was a note by the phone. This was written by my eldest son, David. It said, "Call Dr. Jack Grant when you get in." The area code was Pennsylvania, so if I called now, it was almost midnight. Dr. Grant told David it was okay if I called late, so I did. Dr. Grant seemed friendly enough. The conversation started off like several of the others I had had previously this week. This conversation was sounding very similar to the others I had had. Dr. Grant talked in non-specifics about Marines and World War II and finding lost buddies. When I had listened long enough and felt that the conversation was coming to an end, I asked him point-blank if he knew David Dougherty. He did not mention anything about the letter I had sent to him. He said, "Did I *know* him? I practically tucked him in bed each night for two years. I was his squad leader. I was there when he died." I got goose bumps. Pay dirt. I had found him!

We talked about what happened on June 15, 1944. I told him that my dad wasn't convinced that the body buried in Hawthorne, New Jersey, was that of David. Dad felt his body must have been lost in Saipan. Dr. Grant stopped me cold. He wanted me to tell my dad that David was killed by a mortar; the amphibious tractor carrying the squad turned around and headed back to the LST with five dead and three seriously wounded. Sergeant Grant assured me that David's body was handed off to responsible hands and properly identified. His body was not lost.

I did not realize at the time the nerve I hit. I was aware that Marines stuck together. *Semper fidelis* is not just a motto. I have read that Marines would risk their lives in battle to retrieve their wounded or dead. A squad or platoon leader felt even more responsibility in this area.

Sergeant Grant also told me that two years earlier in 1992, he had decided to try to find the remaining members of his squad. They had all been separated after the aborted landing. He did find all of them and they had been having annual reunions. They sounded like private solemn occasions. Sergeant Grant said he would send me the addresses of the remaining squad and would alert them to my pending inquiries. I told Sergeant Grant that my dad, a fellow World War II Marine veteran, would most likely want to communicate directly with him. I thanked him for his time and said goodbye. I was excited and grateful.

I couldn't wait to tell Dad, but it would have to wait until tomorrow. I realized I was treading on some thin ice here. By the tone of Dr. Grant's voice, I could tell that this was sacred territory to him also. I knew as well that this news would be received by Dad with mixed emotions. I did call him the next day when I was at work. Dad was outside. Mom called him in. I told him that I had located and talked to David L. Dougherty's squad leader, a Sergeant Jack Grant. He was a dentist now living in Pennsylvania and had relocated the rest of the squad. I told Dad he wanted very much to talk to him. Dad was silent for a moment and then said, "Oh...?" It was obvious Dad was very emotional and perhaps conflicted about this. I gave him Jack Grant's phone number and told him to give him a call. It took Dad the better part of a week, but he did call and made contact. It was quite a positive experience.

Jack Grant sent me information on the remaining squad, and I received letters from Leo Kelly, Charlie Wolf, and William Hewitt, as well a picture of the squad and a short letter from Sergeant Grant. It turned out that William Hewitt was on my first list of 15 that John Stone had given me. He called Jack Grant before he wrote me. After all the years, it seemed the PFCs and corporals still needed permission from their sergeant to respond to my letter. I also sent a letter of thanks to John Stone, letting him know thanks to his diligence we had been successful.

On May 29, 1995, I received a letter from William L. Hewitt.

"Dr. Jamieson,

In reference to David Dougherty...He and I were in the same squad and was friendly, but not close buddies. I was a group leader, along with Carter and Kelly. My group consisted of Wolf, Arthur, and Simpkins. You might find out more by writing to Carter or Kelly.

About our landing in Saipan, I remember it being Yellow Beach, but not which one. Can't remember much. I was hit with shrapnel in the amtrac in my left shoulder, got out in shallow water, and was ran over by the same amtrac. Right leg and right foot. Twenty-one years later, shrapnel worked its way into my left lung and was taken out. They had to take out 2/3 of it. Can't be of much help.

I'll give you some addresses; hope you find what you want."

And I got a letter from Leo Kelly:

"June 9, 1995.

Dear Dr. Jamieson,

Sorry I haven't written to you sooner. We have been out on vacation. Right after the war, Mr. and Mrs. Dougherty wrote me and I gave them as much information about their son as I could at that time. I will try to tell you now as much as I can remember. I am now 74 years old. It's been a long time.

All the members of our squad were like brothers. We really looked out for each other. We went on liberty together (very seldom) and shared all our problems. On your map about the landing at Saipan. We never landed. We were supposed to hit Yellow 2. We got hung up on coral about 100 feet offshore between Yellow 2 and 3, when mortar rounds exploded overhead, wounding and knocking out everyone in the amtrac. When I came to, I checked men and driver, who was out, and found most of the squad either dead or seriously wounded. Only Bill Hewitt and I were able to get out of the amtrac and into water. We were able to stand up. We went behind the amtrac to look at beach. Shells and rifle fire hit all around us. At this time, the driver of the amtrac woke up and came back, running over Bill and me. Lucky for me, I went under the amtrac. Bill was not so lucky. He was run over by tread, ripping his leg and arm. I pulled Bill ashore, and we laid on a small strip of sand when firing stopped. I went down the beach to Yellow 3, found a medic and two others. They put me on a stretcher and went back for Bill. I can tell you that those killed in the amtrac didn't know what hit them. They died instantly. I rejoined my squad two days before they went aboard ship for Iwo Jima. I can only remember Carter being there. On the fifth day at Iwo, I was wounded again. Mortar round wounded in shoulders and back. On the way back to the beach, I was shot in both legs, taken to the hospital ship, then flown to Hawaii hospital Aiea Heights. Then back to San Diego Hospital. Last year, we visited Hawaii on Maui. At our old camp, the 4th Marine Division has built a park and shrine in honor of all Marines that served in the 4th. About the dysentery, David and a few others, sick as dogs and feeling worse, were really happy to be going to the hospital. They on their return to the squad told us about getting liberty and what they saw and did. No one else, as I can remember, got liberty because we were getting ready for Saipan. When we went on liberty in San Diego and Los Angeles, David and Jack Jones, James Samson and myself always went out together. Sometimes we had dates and if not, we ate and drank beer. We always were looking for good food. Enclosed is a picture of our squad, names on the back. For 50 years, I thought only Hewitt and myself survived. Then three years ago, Jack Grant called me on phone saying he had found some of our squad. We have been getting together for a little reunion at least once a year since. This year, it will be October 6 at Charlie Wolf's, Ocean City, New Jersey. He and his wife own an apartment building. We expect seven of our squad to be there. Hope this letter helps a little.

Sincerely,

Leo Kelly."

And finally, Charlie Wolf had the most prolific letter and memory of his experiences with his squad.

"Dear Dr. Jamieson,

We were a rifle squad in C Company 25th Marines 1st Battalion 4th Marine Division stationed at Camp LeJeune in North Carolina. Toward the end of our training we boarded ship and proceeded to sail south and passed through the Panama Canal and on up to Camp Pendleton. We left ship via landing craft and made a practice landing on the shores of California midway between San Diego and Los Angeles. We relocated to a tent camp. This was a place we would call home until shortly after Christmas 1943. There was nothing but tents in a canyon called Las Pulgas. (*Editor's note: Spanish for The Fleas*) I vividly recall the cold showers and the very cold toilet seats. I recall going on liberty with my friend David Dougherty. We hitchhiked up to Los Angeles. We did not go browsing around. Instead we went to a local barber shop - got a hair cut and proceeded to have him give us a mud pack facial. Can't you imagine - two marines getting a facial. Believe me, after spending our last several months at the tent camp in Las Pulgas Canyon, we needed a facial.

Shortly after our L.A. liberty the 25th Marines moved to San Diego. I remember our last night at the tent camp. It was hectic. We had our rifles and we had ammo. I recall shooting my BAR (Browning automatic rifle) through the roof of our tent. When we arrived at San Diego we went aboard ships. We were there for a few days. We had liberty in San Diego. Some of us did not drink. We were all too young. David and I went to a roller skating rink. No big deal. We were trying to make out with the young ladies at the roller skating rink. Had no luck.

We finally sailed out of San Diego and headed toward our first combat landing. We were the first troops to leave the U.S. and proceed directly to combat. Around the end of January 1944 we landed on the Marshall Islands. Our company assaulted a small island just off the main objective of Roi-Namur. I do not even remember the real name of the island. Its code name was Boggerlap. We landed a day prior to the assault on Roi-Namur. Roi was a small island. Almost the entire island was used as a Japanese air strip. Roi was attached to another island called Namur via a causeway. Our landing the day before the main landing on Roi-Namur was to capture the island so that artillery could be brought ashore to support the main landing on Roi-Namur. We were the first U.S. troops to occupy territory previously under Japanese rule. All went well except for a Japanese aircraft which flew over and dropped a few bombs on our little island. We all came through OK.

These islands were part of the Kwajalen Atoll in the Marshall Islands. After the islands were secured we moved over to Namur and waited for replacement garrison troops to arrive. I recall one of our guys, Sammy

Samson, had his foxhole next to a big Japanese bomb. He placed his shelter half over his foxhole and tied the end of it to a ring on the end of the bomb. He had a piece of chalk and wrote on the bomb "Sleep tight." We finally were relieved and boarded ship and sailed back to our base on Maui. Maui was great. The people on Maui treated us as "their Marines." We did some more training at Maui and received a few replacements. Then we were moved over to Pearl Harbor where we boarded LSTs (landing ship tank and *Editor's note: also dubbed by GIs as **Long Slow Targets***). We had quite a few LSTs and were tied up next to one another at a place in Pearl Harbor called West Lock. Each LST had about twenty fifty gallon drums of fuel stored on the front end of the LST. I recall very vividly one Sunday afternoon. David and I were down in the tank deck control room. We had just ripped off a gallon can of apricots from the Navy. Can't you imagine — there we were — with a big open can of apricots; a large tablespoon full of apricots when boom — the LST two ships away from us exploded. I do not know why and I am fairly sure that no one really does know what caused it, anyway, since we were all tied up together the flames jumped from one LST to the others. We cut the lines tying us to the other ships and floated away from the danger. I think five LSTs were destroyed. About a week later we sailed out of Pearl Harbor enroute to Saipan.

We were the first wave going into Saipan. We were in amtracs. On the way in we saw a Navy aircraft get shot down and the pilot bailed out. We could see splashes from Japanese artillery hitting in front of our amtrac. We continued in. About 100 yards from shore we were on the coral reef when disaster struck. The Japanese artillery and/or mortars got the range and hit our amtrac.

It was devastating. Killed were David Dougherty, Sammy Sampson, Jack Jones and several other Marines not part of our squad. They were from D company which was a weapons company. I may have missed some of the other guys. Kelly, Hewitt and myself exited the amtrac. We got behind the amtrac when suddenly the amtrac backed up on us. It ran over Hewitt's leg — Kelly went right under the middle of the amtrac and popped up OK in front of it. I was kicking at the left track as it came back at me. I lost my BAR and landed on Saipan with a machete in one hand and a hand grenade in the other hand. I used one of my hand grenades on a Japanese machine gun emplacement at the end of a small trench dug by the Japanese as a fire lane. The Japanese gunner stopped firing. I went on ahead; caught up with our company commander (Capt. Tom Clarke). Since I had no rifle, Captain Clarke gave me his carbine. There I was with a little carbine and only one magazine of carbine ammo. Captain Clarke was later killed.

Later I was running across a field with another Marine named Martens. The Japanese artillery zeroed in on us. I was wounded and Martens was killed. I crawled back and encountered four Marines who carried me back. I have no idea who they were. They carried me on a poncho. I had lost a lot of blood and was almost unconscious but I heard one of them say "This guy is dead weight." I will never forget David Dougherty. He was a fine young Marine. I and all the other guys are proud to have served with him. When I go to church on Sunday I pray for Dougherty, Jones, Samson, Martens along with all my other KIA buddies.

I was evacuated back to Oahu where I was hospitalized at a US Naval Hospital located at Aiea Heights on Oahu. Officially it was Naval Hospital #10. There I met up with Jack Grant, our squad leader and several other guys. I was on crutches and went to another ward. I had heard that one of our squad was there. His name was Lance LaLancette. He was shocked to see me. He thought that I had been killed.

An interesting thing occurred just a few years ago. The 4th Marine Division had a reunion on the West Coast. After the reunion many of us went to Maui to see our camp site. While there we visited the headquarters of the Pacific Fleet Marine Force. I was talking to the commanding general of the Pacific Fleet Marine Force. I told him that his headquarters looked very familiar. He said that it had been Hospital Navy #10."

Signed,

Charles Wolf."

Jack Grant said that he had a special connection with David Dougherty. "He was 'the kid' in the squad, the youngest and I felt a special need to look out for him." After the war was over and peace was declared, Jack visited the parents of his fallen comrades. He noted that David's parents were completely overwhelmed and distraught with the loss of their only child, but they extended gracious hospitality towards him. He says he was treated like a son and he said it was rough to witness their grief and pain. (My dad, living in nearby Paterson, New Jersey at the time, was not informed of the visit.)

Later on Jack returned to David and Agnes Dougherty's home with his wife, Nancy and she too felt the warmth that they radiated. Agnes made soft bed slippers for their daughter, Nancy Gene, as a gift.

Armed with all this information, I was able to piece together the final moments of Sergeant Grant's squad. Almost instantly killed by the mortar were David Dougherty, Jack Jones and James "Sammy" Sampson. Seriously injured were Pierre LaLancett, Sgt. Grant (lacerated jugular vein), and Harold Metzel. Leo Kelly was miraculously uninjured although run over by the reversing amtrac and ended up carrying the less fortunate Bill

Hewitt to shore whose leg and foot were run over by the amtrac. Leo went on to fight on Saipan and then on Iwo Jima and was wounded there. The adrenalinized Charlie Wolf charged the beach with a grenade in one hand and a machete in the other, in what sounded like the ultimate act of defiance against the enemy, only later to be seriously wounded and near death. Charlie took out a Japanese pill box with the grenade on the way in. John Carter missed the landing with his squad that day as he was on ship recovering from appendicitis. He arrived a few days later and was wounded. Sergeant Grant lost track of Arthur Yancy and John Dewine but recently found out that both survived the War, Dewine without even a scratch. John Simpkins also survived the landing and then went on to Iwo Jima and was wounded there.

This squad of 13 men had trained together at Camp Pendleton, fought together on Roi Namur in the Marshalls, retrained on Maui and was on the first wave on amphibious tractors attempting to land on the invasion of Saipan. These men sacrificed their lives so other Marines could advance to victory. And in one instant the two year band of brothers was changed forever. Most of the survivors waited almost fifty years to find out there were 10 of the squad still alive.

With all this information in mind, our trip was just about ready to go. I had made arrangements to meet with government officials on the island of Saipan. Dad and I would leave in mid-June out of San Francisco, then on to Hawaii and a short stay in Guam, but our first real visit would be Okinawa for the reunion celebration. We would then fly back to Guam and then take a short hop over to Saipan to visit the battle sites and the governor. We would return to Guam. We would finish up our trip in Oahu, where we would visit the Pearl Harbor memorial.

Roger stands on the sculptured Sugar Loaf Hill at the approximate
location where he aided his private.

Roger and SSgt. Jerry Johnson, USMC, pose on top of Sugar Loaf Hill during ceremonies.

"...Having met men like.... Roger Jamieson, if they activated the 6th Marine Division, I'd ask for a transfer. I would have volunteered to be in his unit any day."

SSgt. Jerry Johnson, USMC and Okinawa 50th anniversary reunion tour guide.

CHAPTER 9

Okinawa Plus Fifty: Retaking Sugar Loaf Hill

Dad and I boarded a plane in San Francisco, flew to Hawaii, re-boarded and flew to Guam. During our flight, when we reached midnight, it was June 18, which just so happened to be Father's Day and my dad's birthday. The celebration, 35,000 feet above the Central Pacific, was short lived as we crossed the International Date Line four hours later and it was June 19. We stayed at a little hotel near the airport and tried to get some sleep. We woke up early due to jet lag and went to the airport and got on an airplane and flew to Okinawa. Fifty years earlier on this day, June 19, 1945, Dad left Okinawa on a hospital ship for Guam. Today we were heading from Guam to Okinawa on a commercial jet. When we landed, we had no connections to get to the hotel. A nice Air Force sergeant realizing our situation drove us to Kadena Air Force Base and found us a taxi to the hotel where the tour was staying. The tour didn't start until the following day.

That following day there were several tours we were able to take. We visited the landing beaches and also took a tour of Motobu Peninsula (Northern Okinawa), where Dad had fought.

The next day anybody who was interested in seeing Sugar Loaf Hill was invited to an informal tour. As you have read earlier in this book, Sugar Loaf Hill on May 14, 1945, was the site of a fierce 10-day battle to take the western anchor of what was called the Shuri Line. The Japanese were holed in, literally hiding and replacing losses through an intricate series of caves and tunnels. The objective of the 6th Marine Division was to "take the hill."

It was here where my father volunteered for front-line duty and fought and helped to hold the hill the evening of May 14 until the nine surviving Marines were called off the hill at dawn on May 15. Dad left the hill wounded; he had lost his entire platoon, and one of the main purposes for returning to Okinawa was for Dad to revisit Sugar Loaf Hill and "face his demons." Sugar Loaf Hill is located a few miles north of Naha, the capital city. Several weeks before we had embarked on our trip, Dad and I had learned that Sugar Loaf Hill was to be plowed away to make room for a new shopping mall. After the war, the hill and the surrounding acreage north of the hill (known as Hell's Half-Acre) became base housing for Marines. During the tour, we met a young man who grew up as a Marine's son during the Vietnam era. He had lived on the base and played on Sugar Loaf Hill.

The news that the hill was to be destroyed was depressing to Dad and me. We both knew Dad needed to walk on the hill. Good news came. The United States Marine Corps stationed on Okinawa heard about the plans for destruction. They knew the importance of that hill. Over 2600 U.S. Marines had been killed or wounded on and around it. In fact, it is calculated that the battle represented the most warriors ever killed per square foot: the densest loss of life in battle ever recorded in World War II.[11]

We found out that the move to save Sugar Loaf Hill from the bulldozer was spearheaded by USMC Captain Mark Roberts, with the assistance of his Okinawan wife. He had worked with Okinawa government officials for 2 plus years to not only save the hill, but convert it to a memorial park. Dad had an opportunity at the end of our stay in Okinawa to personally thank Mark for his efforts.

Our tour guides were active or retired Navy and USMC. These guides had spent an entire year preparing to be tour guides. They took classes on the history of the battles and read several books, including Feifer's Tennozan. So when the veterans returned, the guides were very excited to meet the real heroes. Staff Sergeant Jerry Johnson led the expedition to Sugar Loaf. The bus had about 26 people on it, mostly Marines. SSgt. Johnson and the other guide, a former Marine (now missionary), knew the significance of Sugar Loaf Hill. Jerry thought we might have trouble getting on the site, as it was now a gated, closed construction area. As our bus approached the area, Jerry and the minister got out and approached the closed gate. An animated hand-gesturing conversation ensued. We couldn't hear what was being said, but it was apparent the guides were not getting much cooperation from the guards and of course, there was a language barrier to cross also; thus the exaggerated hand gestures. Jerry and the missionary came back on the bus and announced we were not allowed passage. The guards said they were concerned we might get hurt climbing up the hill. The bus was silent and Dad quipped back, "Funny — the Japanese didn't seem concerned about us getting hurt the first time we tried climbing the hill." That brought the bus to laughter and lightened up a little tension.

SSgt. Johnson would not be deterred. He had Plan B already worked out. During his year of study, he had been on and around Sugar Loaf Hill several times. He had anticipated this roadblock and the night before he had done a little reconnaissance. Under the safety of darkness, SSgt. Johnson had taken a flashlight and wire clippers and took a quarter-mile hike from the south side of the hill to the fence line that separated the construction site and the hill from the adjacent properties. He had cut down a section of fence. So we put the bus in reverse, went back out on Highway 1, proceeded south for half a mile, and then turned left and parked at an apartment complex. During this maneuver, I got in a conversation with one of the tour guides, the former Marine, now minister. I told him that Dad had fought on Sugar Loaf and saw Major Courtney fall. The minister realized the historical significance of this and asked my dad if it was true. What I didn't realize until then was that Dad was quite worked up emotionally at this point. He answered yes, but was quite shaky and his voice quivered. If I had been sensitive and known Dad's emotional state at that point, I wouldn't have said what I had said. It turned out on this small side tour that Dad was the only veteran who had fought on the hill.

We got out of the bus. We were now going to break the law and trespass. This would be the second time that Dad climbed Sugar Loaf without the approval of the Japanese government. It heightened the whole experience.

We hiked down a narrow dirt path with some scrub-brush on each side. There was a barbed-wire fence line neatly cut by recon SSgt. Jerry Johnson. We walked through, and there it was - the reverse slope of Sugar Loaf Hill. Dad remarked to Jerry and me that he had never got to see the back side of the hill before.

We made our way up the hill to the top and Dad was noticeably emotional and shaky. We stopped and looked around. To the north was the flats called Hell's Half-Acre. It was a construction site, now neatly excavated. Two small hills remained, Queen Hill, and to the east of that was Charlie Hill. Behind Sugar Loaf to the southeast was Half-Moon Hill and to the direct southwest, Horseshoe Hill. When the Marines had fought in 1945, Sugar Loaf was considered by the Japanese military strategists as the western anchor of the Shuri defense line. The two taller hills that flanked its posterior, Horseshoe and Half-Moon, gave a great vantage point from which to observe US troop movements and to shoot cannons and mortars. We stood and took it all in. In the process of saving Sugar Loaf Hill from the excavators, much shaving and grooming of the original hill had taken place. Now the northern base of the hill had a 10-foot tall cement foundation. The northern slope was smooth and at the top it had been leveled off and asphalted to accommodate what would be a water tower/shrine. Cement stairs and railings had been placed to make it easier for visitors to climb.

The hill was now a stylized monument of its previous rugged form, but nonetheless it <u>was</u> Sugar Loaf Hill. It was a sterilized version of what Dad remembered fifty years ago, when dead Marines lay strewn side by side over the 2 and a half acres. The fighting on that hill had been so ferocious and continuous that the dead could not be collected until the hill had been secured for the final time. Dad found the spot, based on his memory of helping hold the west flank of the hill, where he fought, where he aided his wounded, dying private. The experience was a good one and fitting that it was a small informal party of Marines. Later in the week there would be a large ceremony with dignitaries and high-ranking military and hundreds of guests. That was an important visit too, but I know Dad was quite relieved to have visited it first this way.

Dad's countenance was much lighter as we marched off the hill and back to the buses. We all sat down and somebody blurted out, "I'd like to thank Sergeant ("...soon to be Corporal..." someone interrupted) Johnson for the well-executed secret mission." We all laughed and clapped for Sgt. Johnson's excellent private tour.

Peace Park, Mabuni Cliffs, Okinawa

CHAPTER 10

Dad's 15 Minutes of Fame

On June 23, 1995, the tour group boarded several buses to travel to the southern tip of Okinawa - the Mabuni Cliffs. I might say at this point that I had never imagined that bus rides with seventy and eighty years olds could be so entertaining. I had figured back when we were planning the trip that the travel time would be boring. Nothing could have been further from the truth. Many of the veterans had left there wives at home. (Or perhaps I should say, most of the wives decided to wisely stay at home for a much needed respite). Most of the veterans were NCOs. They were rowdy and boisterous and very funny; name calling, Bronx cheers and the like. Dad and I were belly laughing most of the trip on the bus with these veterans. These men became teenagers again.

So off to Mabuni we go. It was about a 2 hour ride. This is where the last battle for Okinawa was fought. The Japanese and several civilians jumped to their deaths rather than surrender. The Japanese, out of a nationalistic sense of honor and pride, would jump. The Okinawans jumped for fear of worse reprisal from the Americans. The Japanese had convinced many of the locals that the U.S. troops were savages. Here, 50 years later, the Okinawans erected a beautiful peace park. The name of every person killed in the 84-day battle was etched in marble. The concentric walls were arranged in accordion style. The names of all 150,000 Okinawans, 90,000 Japanese, and 12,000 U.S. Marines, Soldiers and Sailors were on the walls. This island battle represented the most lives lost in the Pacific theatre. On our way to the peace park, we traveled over Mezado Ridge. This is the area where Dad encountered a sniper's bullet on his way to rejoin the 22nd Marines after he had recovered from Sugar Loaf Hill. Although Dad could not pinpoint the exact spot, he was familiar with the general surroundings.

The ceremony, one of several we had and would attend, had its own flavor.

This was a solemn occasion for the Japanese and Okinawans. Most of the speakers were long-winded without interpreters. Traditional Japanese music played over the loud speaker. The Marine tour group stood quietly perched slightly above the memorial park and patiently listened. We were waiting for the ceremony to be completed when we would be allowed to find the names of fallen Marines. We brought rubbing paper and pencils. When the ceremony was over, we moved down to the U.S. section of the walls. I found Major Henry Courtney's name. This was the one Dad wanted. As you recall from previous chapters, Major Courtney was the Marine that was killed at the crest of Sugar Loaf Hill leading a charge. He had received the Medal of Honor for his bravery and valor. I began rubbing the name, when I noticed a large TV camera at ground level pointing at my hands and Major Courtney's name. I then noticed multiple still cameras snapping away. A crowd had surrounded Dad and me. We had not expected anything like this would happen. I finished my work and stood up. Dad and I were almost pinned up against the wall. A well-groomed, handsome young Japanese man was standing by the TV video camera. He politely asked what we were doing. He had no accent. I explained that Dad was a World War II Marine veteran of the Battle of Sugar Loaf Hill and he had seen Major Courtney die that night, so he turned to my dad and began asking him questions. He asked four questions. The first had to do with current Japanese-American diplomatic relations (currently there was a struggle going on over the U.S. Military presence on Okinawa). Dad was keenly aware that Governor Ota (a child survivor of the battle 50 years ago) was a pacifist and was petitioning the central government of Japan to push the Marines, Navy, Air Force, and Army out of Okinawa. Dad knew the significance and repercussions of that if it were to occur. The Philippines had recently been successful in pushing out the American military presence in their country. Okinawa now had an even more vital strategic importance. So he attempted to explain to the interviewer what he felt. Dad said, "I feel the local government and the military on Okinawa should come to agreement. I think they need each other, although I hope defense of Okinawa will never be necessary". It was vintage Dad, the contract negotiator / English major, hoping both countries could work together, etc., etc. It was somewhat of a boring answer. The interviewer asked two more questions of equal value; these were general-type questions, which were intended to relax Dad a bit and he forgot he was talking to a camera, and he began conversing with the impromptu interview. Then the final question, "Sir, when you look around this memorial park and you see all the names of the fallen, how does it make you feel?" My dad stopped and said, "It gives us all pause-..." He broke down and cried. He took off his glasses to wipe his eyes and motioned his hands toward the camera, "Stop the wars…I'm sorry." My Dad was a very reserved and private man but the enormity of the memorial wall and all the names caused him to think about all the kids he had seen killed. He was a Marine officer. He didn't cry very often and not in public, for sure. With that, the camera shut off, the interviewers asked my dad's name, to which he replied, "Walter Jamieson". In a formal identification setting Dad used his first name. The reporter then asked my dad's rank and branch of service and turned around and began to walk away. The small crowd dissipated. I called out to the interviewer and said, "Excuse me— who are you?" He stopped and turned around and said, "I'm James Hattori with CBS News." Dad turned to me and said quietly, "Oh, shit." We both knew which sound bite, if any, would make the final cut.

Dad was also interviewed by Stars and Stripes and was very thorough in his answers.

The following day, on June 24, 1995, was a dedication ceremony at Sugar Loaf Hill. The ceremony that day included the Commandant of the United States Marine Corps, General Monday, Walter Mondale, and several Japanese dignitaries and World War II veterans from both sides. We hiked up the stairs. There was a pleasant young lady who spotted Dad and came right up to him and said, "Mr. Jamieson, you're a star." Joan Gilbertson was a CBS producer and handed Dad her card and informed him that in fact, Dad would be featured on CBS Nightly News with Dan Rather that night. Joan wanted him interviewed again on Sugar Loaf Hill, but Dad deferred. We found Wendell Majors, a Sugar Loaf Hill veteran from the same night, who took the next interview. He did a fantastic job and his segment showed the next evening, on Saturday night, on CBS News. Both CBS Nightly News TV interviews are available for you to view on a link to You Tube at www.onceamarinebook.info

We later called Mom and gave her a heads-up so that she could record the segment on the VCR. It turned out to be a great segment, and Dad's "Stop the wars" statement, coming from a wounded, battle-hardened World War II Marine officer, capped off the whole piece (my hand even made it on the clip for 4 seconds). Friends of Mom and Dad, from coast to coast, unaware that we were even over in Okinawa, saw the clip and called Mom in California to give her a heads-up. My brother Douglas later commented that he didn't realize Dad was against war. As Dad would say later, anyone who has been in battle is against war. He fought with the hope that his children and grandchildren would never have to go to war. Dad was hawkish on being prepared for war but he personally distained war.

Marine Officer Roger Jamieson and Japanese Army Officer Shizuo
Uizumi, former Sugar Loaf Hill foes, now friends.

Shizuo and Roger shake hands on former battleground,
Sugar Loaf Hill Dedication Ceremony

CHAPTER 11

"My Dear Friend Shizuo,"

After we had made our tour to the Mabuni Cliffs we were both pretty exhausted. It had been a long, hot day of travel. My diary for that day states, "Almost decided not to go to the 'Okinawa Plus Fifty' reception, but glad we did." Each evening there was a dinner program scheduled. That night, we loaded on a bus that went to a large hall where we were greeted at the door by Japanese guests, who immediately handed us a glass of Japanese whiskey. I am not much of a whiskey fan — I took a sip and nodded thanks to be culturally sensitive, then discarded the whiskey when they weren't looking. My dad, who likes Scotch whiskey, said to me that this particular Japanese counterpart was a poor rendition.

There was a stage area above the main hall where several buffet lines of seafood in steamers were open and ready. Hundreds of veterans entered the room, hungry and ready to eat. One Japanese lady, the apparent caterer and hostess, kept trying to keep the World War II veterans at bay, away from the food lines. She was quite upset when she could not control the hungry mob. She told us that we could eat after the program. The banner over the stage read "50 years of Peace and Friendship Commemoration Dinner and Reception" both in English and Japanese, but it looked like World War III was about to erupt. The hungry crowd of Americans standing around the sumptuous buffet tables of seafood, rice, and salad was restless. The speakers from Japan rambled on with interpreters. The World War II American veterans weren't listening. They were talking and eating. The lady in charge of the food line was getting angrier. Then Walter "Fritz" Mondale arrived. He was serving as U.S. Ambassador to Japan under then-President Bill Clinton. He made his royal entry onto the stage. I don't think anyone briefed him on the theme of the evening. He looked out on the crowd of U.S. veterans and congratulated them on how they stuck it to the Japanese fifty years ago, "way to go," etc., etc. All this with a banner hanging over him that he could not see declaring "50 years of Peace and Friendship". It was surreal. It would have been appropriate at an American Legion or WFW convention back home, but not here with all the Japanese hosts and veterans. Dad and I shook our heads and couldn't believe our ears, but we got a big chuckle out of it. After the ceremonial aspect of the evening was complete, and the food lines were officially open (most of us had already eaten). A replica big band-era band (current servicemen and women dressed in WWII era military uniforms) played. They were excellent. Dad went outside the hall to the foyer area and began meeting U.S. Marines (active). In the course of his visit to Okinawa, he had managed to meet and talk with a private, a PFC, a corporal, a sergeant, a second lieutenant, a first lieutenant, and a captain; all ranks dad had attained during his 10-year stint in the Marines. He loved talking with the young Marines and Dad had attained some celebrity status being a Sugar Loaf survivor. While Dad was outside the hall, I had noticed a small group of Japanese men in the hall. They were wearing name tames that said "62nd Imperial Army." They were huddled all by themselves. I said hello to them. Most could not speak any English, but we shook hands and smiled. One older gentleman was wearing a beret. He was a professor in the Japanese university system. He spoke English. He told me that he was a kamikaze pilot. I asked him how he was still alive. He said as he was flying his suicide mission to Okinawa, he began to think about all this and he had second thoughts. So he flew around until he ran out of gas and feathered his plane into the ocean just offshore. He swam in, raised his hands and surrendered. I got some of these Japanese veterans' autographs on the title page of my copy of Tennozan. One gentleman spoke English very well and had a beer in one hand and held a cigarette in the other. He wore a nice dinner jacket and was handsome and well groomed. We talked for a few moments and I asked him to wait right there… "Don't move." He just seemed particularly friendly to me. I found Dad and told him I wanted him to meet someone. Dad came in and I introduced him to Shizuo Uizumi. Shizuo shook hands with Dad and noticed my dad was a U.S. Marine. He said in a Japanese accent, "Oh, you are Marine….. You are TOUGH!" My dad said, "Well, you're 62nd Imperial Army; you are TOUGH!" They both laughed a bit. My dad asked Shizuo where he fought. Shizuo said, "Sugar Loaf Hill." My dad said, "So did I." My dad asked, "What did you shoot?" Shizuo replied, "A cannon." My father retorted, "A cannon? All I had was a little pea shooter!" It turned out that both men were the same age and lieutenants at the time.

I took a picture of the two men and they exchanged addresses. It was a magical moment and one that I had not expected to happen. Two former enemies who fought on opposite sides at Sugar Loaf Hill were now shaking hands. We left that night and I thanked Shizuo for not hitting my dad with his cannon — although who knows, my dad was hit by shrapnel in the arm that night by a large explosive. Dad would later learn (through correspondence) that Shizuo had grown up in China, where his Japanese parents did business. Shizuo learned English at an American Christian missionary school. When World War II broke out, Shizuo's father was not happy. He knew the Americans and he knew Japan would eventually lose.

Dad and Shizuo met again the next day. We found him standing on Sugar Loaf Hill before the official ceremony. He was holding a rising sun battle flag with many Japanese names written on it. I pointed this out to Dad and he walked over and shook Shizuo's hand and smiled. What followed was a reporter and cameramen's feeding frenzy. Here were Dad and Shizuo, shaking hands on an old battleground, now friends. A nice article and picture later appeared in the Leatherneck magazine as well as the Marine Corps local publication, "Okinawa Marine."

The ceremony on Sugar Loaf that day was well done. Representatives from both countries were there. This was the final ceremony and it was as if Sugar Loaf became the focal point and symbol for the entire 50th anniversary reunion tour. A Marine colonel prefaced the ceremony with a solemn appeal to the audience to remember that we were all standing on sacred ground and to respect the ceremony. Then Commandant Monday gave a speech. Fritz Mondale had earlier made his grand entrance up the hill, back slapping, smiling, happy and hand shaking every thing in sight. You'd have thought it was the 1984 Democratic National Convention. The Ambassador this time did, in all fairness, give an excellent speech. He hit a home run and captured the moment. The Japanese speakers also did a wonderful job.

The 6th Marine Division Association left a plaque on the hill. It read as follows:

SUGAR LOAF

A SACRED SITE

NOW A PEACEFUL PLACE

This is the summit of Sugar Loaf Hill, site of the costliest single battle in U.S. Marine Corps history and hallowed ground for the two nations which fought here. Casualties of the Sixth Marine Division and Navy supporting personnel totaled 2,662 killed or wounded during the period from May 12 to 21, 1945. Anti Tank, automatic weapons, mortar and artillery fire was so fierce an additional 1,289 Marines suffered battle fatigue. In the fury of the crossfire 600 Okinawan civilians also lost their lives.

The ferocity of the battle involved every type of relentless firepower and use of heavily fortified caves, which made it impossible to record the number of Japanese casualties. (Ultimately the Japanese 32nd Army lost some 90,000 men on Okinawa).

The fighting was so intense that Marines captured and lost the hill four times in one day. Heroism was common on both sides. American historians have compared the Battle of Sugar Loaf Hill to the Battle of Gettysburg during the United States Civil War.

Sugar Loaf Hill, flanked by Half Moon and Horseshoe Hills, as they were called by Marines of the 6th Division, anchored the superb Shuri defense lines of General Mitsuru Ushijima. The extremely difficult American victory here, led by General Lemuel C. Shepard Jr., opened the way to the end of the island battle on June 21, 1945. It was World War II's last land battle.

Historians agree that it cost more lives that any other island battle in the Pacific. Most of the lives were civilian. In the end, some 150,000 Okinawans (one third of their population) died as the result of the fighting.

Sugar Loaf Hill should endure as a monument to peace. It will be preserved in the minds of 6th Division Marines and Navy Corpsmen who participated as a supreme test of courage and faith in one another. Survivors from both nations treasure its soil as a symbol of courageous warriors. Their spirit roams the hills.

The Sixth Marine Division Association

United States of America

June 23, 1995

The Sixth Marine Division's only combat mission was Okinawa and it's baptism of fire led them straight through Sugar Loaf Hill.

Dad and Shizuo corresponded for about a year after meeting, exchanging Christmas greetings and more importantly thoughts about World War II and being an officer. In one letter, Shizuo told of on an incident he had on Okinawa while a 1st Lieutenant. He and his men were holed up in a cave and under attack by Marines. He had received orders to lead a Bonzai charge (a last ditch certain suicide raid). He disobeyed orders and kept his men in the cave. They all survived the battle and the war. They still meet together with their families during reunions. Shizuo asked my dad if he was wrong to disobey orders like that. This incident had bothered him all these years and now he was asking a fellow officer for advice.

Dad wrote,

"My Dear Friend, Shizuo,

"Concerning your survival and your five men, it is easy for me to tell you what I think of that. First, I would have done the same thing myself; you not only did nothing wrong, you did every thing right. You were a platoon leader in your own tradition – you told your men to stay alive and you would take the responsibility. That absolved them of any false blame or guilt and established the high caliber of your own courage and intelligence. Every year, when the six families meet, it is a reaffirmation of the fact that Lieutenant Oizumi was a good man who did the right thing. I, for one, salute you."

Sincerely,

Roger Jamieson

Those are powerful words from a veteran World War II Marine officer. But Dad respected Shizuo and was honored that he would share, officer to officer, about his dilemma. Dad's response was sincere and true.

Most U.S. veterans that I met on Okinawa had made peace with themselves and the enemy they had fought and hated fifty years earlier. I had interviewed some veterans stateside who had not been able to bury the hatchet. I don't stand in judgment of these vets. I did not walk in their boots. It was, however, obvious to me that Dad had been able to let it go. In the same letter, Dad shared these thoughts with Shizuo. "My wife, Betty, asked me before I left for the reunion tour how I might react if I met the Japanese Okinawan veterans there. I told her I didn't know; I'd have to get there and find out. My reaction, I am certain, spoke for itself; I quickly was imbued with the very idea of the reunion and the spirit of it. It was inspiring to observe veterans of both sides there to celebrate the fact that that was the last battle of the war and to realize that both nations are indeed friends today…Such thoughts made it a most natural result for us to meet, shake hands, and, without saying it, signify that you and I are now friends. We are, as we both know, two very lucky friends to have survived and now to have met."

Roger and Shizuo became friends and developed a mutual admiration: former foes and former warriors. After about a year of correspondence, Dad lost contact with Shizuo and never heard from him again. But their short lived friendship was a blessing to both men.

Acting Governor Borja signs declaration of David L. Dougherty Day,
June 26, 1995 as Jay and Roger look on. Photo courtesy of
Donovan Brooks, Pacific Stars and Stripes

Fallen hero remembered, David L. Dougherty. Photo courtesy of
Donovan Brooks, Pacific Stars and Stripes.

CHAPTER 12

Visiting Saipan

Some time in May 1995, a little before all the information was coming in on David Leslie Dougherty's squad, I wrote a letter to the governor of Saipan, letting him know that my father and I would be visiting the island. I explained to the governor, Mr. Tenario, that my dad's cousin was killed on June 15, 1944, while landing on Saipan. I also asked the governor if he would proclaim the day of our visit, June 26, 1995, as David Leslie Dougherty Day in honor of my dad's cousin and all of the men who fell to liberate Saipan. I received a letter back from him that he "saw no problem" with such a declaration and referred us to his public information officer, Nancy Weil, for all the details.

When we arrived on Saipan on the evening of June 25, 1995, we rented a car and went to our hotel near Yellow 2, the beach where David Leslie Dougherty's squad attempted to land. We stayed at a nice hotel, The Pacific Garden, that night and we ate at the outdoor seafood buffet right on the landing beach. The food was fabulous and then the disco music started. About 30 Japanese college students were dancing and singing karaoke and having a good time. Dad and I sat and soaked it all in.

Saipan is a U.S. protectorate. It reminded me a lot of the Philippines. I had lived in the Philippines in 1986 and 1987 as a medical missionary with my wife and three small boys. Saipan was financially sounder than the Philippines, less crowded, and there was no pollution.

I was thinking as we sat there in the open-air restaurant on the beach that fifty years and 11 days ago, this area was pure mayhem. The lagoon, according to locals we talked to who had been there, was "red with spilled blood". Two generations later, so much had changed. Here, now, the grandchildren of the Japanese Army were vacationing, dancing and having fun. Dad's comment on that thought was, "It's fine, but don't let them try it again." I understood.

The following morning, we got up early and found Yellow 2 quite easily, thanks to our research and help from Sergeant Grant's squad. Dad was relieved to see the landing beach where David was killed. He said he would always remember that site. I called Nancy Weil. She apparently got our dates mixed up and thought we were arriving that night. She scrambled and put a program together. We visited with Acting Governor Jesus Borja. Dad was interviewed by Donovan Brooks of the Pacific Stars and Stripes Guam bureau chief. The article made the June 30, 1995 edition of the Stars and Stripes. Governor Borja proclaimed the day David Leslie Dougherty Day and we received some nice photos of the ceremony from Donovan Brooks later. The proclamation read as follows:

DAVID LESLIE DOUGHERTY DAY
JUNE 26.1995
A PROCLAMATION

"The Commonwealth of Northern Mariana Islands enjoys its current status thanks to the ultimate sacrifice of more than 3,000 brave men made 51 years ago. Individual sacrifice for the common good deserves recognition whenever possible.

Private First Class David Leslie Dougherty of the 4th Marine Division was killed in action June 15, 1944.

He received posthumously the Purple Heart, the Presidential Unit Citation, and the Asiatic-Pacific Campaign Medal for his service. NOW, THEREFORE, I, JESUS C. BORJA, Acting Governor of the Commonwealth of the Northern Mariana Islands, by virtue of the authority vested in me by the constitutional laws of the Commonwealth, do hereby proclaim June 26, 1995 as David Leslie Dougherty Day in the Commonwealth.

IN WITNESS WHEREOF I have hereunto set my hand on this 26th day of June 1995.

Signed,
Jesus C. Borja.

After exchange of gifts and handshakes and photo ops, Nancy Weil took us to the Court of Honor, where we laid a wreath and left a picture of David Leslie Dougherty for the war museum with the following inscription: "David Leslie Dougherty, 4th Marine Division, 1-C-25, KAI Saipan, June 15, 1944. He was a good Marine. We loved him and we will never forget him."

Signed,

W.R. Jamieson and family and his squad members from Company C-1-25

In the article that was written about Dad's visit to Saipan, Dad told Mr. Brooks, "David was four years younger than me. Because of frequent family get-togethers, I often saw David. We were as thick as brothers." Dad further commented on visiting where David was killed, "It gives you a sense of relief," Roger Jamieson said with a sigh.[12]

So our business in Saipan was complete. We had visited where David was killed, we had met with the governor, and we had laid a wreath at his memorial. Now it was on to Guam.

Governor Carl T.C. Gutierrez of Guam presents "The Ancient Order of the
Chamorri" award to Roger.

CHAPTER 13

Guam-Where America's Day Begins

In June of 1995, just a week before our trip, I decided to make contact with anyone in the town of Agat, Guam. That was the town the 1st Provisional Marine Brigade liberated in July of 1944. My father, as I had stated before, was appointed liaison officer to Brigadier General Lemuel Shepherd. We had planned to drive around and check out the sights for ourselves, but in a last-minute effort, I decided to write a letter to the mayor of Agat.

My medical office was probably the last clinic in town to obtain a fax machine. My associate, Dr.Greg Thomas, and I were a bit resistant to high tech, but at the urging of my friend and attorney, Rick Stein, ("You really should get a fax.") we bought our first fax machine that June. The first fax I ever sent out was to the mayor's office in Guam. I didn't really know who the mayor was. I can't recall now how I found the fax number, but I did, and I still remember dialing 1-671-565-G-U-A-M. The letter rolled into the machine and came out, the telephone dialed, and soon the familiar high-pitched, creeping, peeping sounds came out indicating apparent connection. I stood there wondering if my letter would really transmit. It was a simple letter. I had introduced myself and explained that my father, a returning USMC veteran of Guam and liaison officer to General Shepherd, was visiting Agat on June 27. While we were there we would like to stop in at the mayor's office and say hello. One week later, approximately 2 days before I was due to leave Salem and link up with my dad in San Francisco to depart, I received a thick manila envelope from Antonio C. Babauta, Mayor of Agat. The packet had many useful pieces of information about Guam, maps, hotels, and the enclosed letter:

June 7, 1995
"Dear Dr. Jamieson:

Thank you for your letter and your plans to visit Agat. Enclosed is information of interest for your visit. I have made arrangements for the governor or lieutenant governor to present to your father, for his kindness and generous contribution to our people and community, the Ancient Order of Chamorri Award and a key to the village. We are also planning for a luncheon at our community center in his honor and his other buddies who sacrificed their lives for your freedom. Our building is right in Agat Bay, better then known as Yellow Beach 2 area during the battle.

Other items of interest are a boat ride in Agat Bay or a hike visit to Japanese lookout point in Thena. We will try our best to ensure that you both enjoy this visit to our small and humble community.

Please let us know what your flight number is and what time you will be arriving on island, as well as other itinerary. If we could be of any other assistance, please don't hesitate to contact me by telephone, fax, or letter. We are looking forward to your visit on June 27.

Sincerely,

Antonio C. Babauta, Mayor of Agat."

What? Ancient Order of the Chamorri Award and key to the city? A luncheon with the governor? I couldn't believe it.

I did worry a little bit about all this, as I knew my dad's personality. He would not want to call attention to himself or take credit for anything to do with the U.S. liberating Guam. But I did tell him what was planned and he took it in stride. Guam would be our second to last stop on our tour.

Each island we visited had its own flavor and personality. Okinawa is a more metropolitan island. The population is larger. The Okinawans have coexisted with the American military presence since 1945, and I would say that there was a distance felt between the local Okinawans and us as we returned there. Saipan had a little warmer personality than Okinawa, but I did sense a small amount of reservation there. Guam, on the other hand, is probably one of the most patriotic, pro-American (they are American) places I have ever visited. Guamanians have not forgotten what the Americans did in liberating them in 1944, especially those who lived through it.

(As a side note, I want to make a comment about the patriotism of Guamanians. Several years earlier, in 1987, I had met two Guamanian brothers, John and Sam Saison, when my wife and I and my three boys did a medical missionary year of service in the Philippines spoken of earlier. The Saison brothers lived on the same mission base as we did. When I learned they were from Guam, I displayed my ignorance when I asked them what their citizenship was. Whoops! Diplomatic mistake. "We are **Americans!**" I heard loud and clear. I found out soon that Guamanians are proud to be Americans, more proud than most of us on the mainland.)

When we arrived back in Guam on June 26, 1995, we stayed at the Inn at the Bay in Agat. We got up early that morning and we talked about the day. While in Okinawa, we bought some Marine mementos and wrapped them up as gifts to give to the mayor, the vice-mayor, and to Governor Carl T.C. Gutierrez of Guam. Dad and I talked over some ideas about an acceptance speech for the award he was to be given. I realized that this ordeal might be an emotional one for Dad, and while he had such a command of the English language, at a time like this, it probably was a good idea to prepare a few talking points. We did this in the hotel early in the morning and headed to the motel's restaurant, where Mayor Babauta had planned to meet us for breakfast. Dad was dressed for work complete with tie.

Tony Babauta was 4 years old when the Japanese invaded his peaceful rural island soon after the attack on Pearl Harbor. The small U.S. military presence was no match for the Japanese army. Soon the Japanese controlled all of Guam. The Guamanians headed for the hills, literally; they left their villages and lived by their wits for 3 years in caves. At night, they would come down to the villages and forage for what they could find and scramble back. Tony remembered all too well what life was like under the brutal military dictatorship of the Japanese. Tony, now 59 years old, was more than the mayor of Agat, as we would see as we toured around that day. In the small island town, he was mentor, chief social worker, and man of peace for his people. He was a kind man. He looked out for the less fortunate in his community, aiding them with food and shelter. He knew everyone in his town.

He met us at the table. His grandchildren had printed paper table mats that said, "HAFA ADAI LT. JAMIESON!!! GUAM WELCOMES YOU TO PARADISE!!!" What a nice touch and that set the tone of hospitality we would experience that day on Guam. After breakfast, Tony took us for a tour. He knew the battle sites. Major General Lemuel Shepherd was the MacArthur of Guam. He, with the help of the Army, Marines, and Navy, liberated the island. Being a liaison officer between the United States Marine Corps and the Army, put my dad in good standing with Tony and all of Guam, it would turn out. Tony knew exactly where Dad landed on the 21st of July 1944, known then as W-Day for Guam. Tony took us to the exact beach where Dad landed. I have video of him talking about what happened. Dad became quite animated when he realized he <u>was</u> at the landing beach. Dad was in the sixth wave landing craft, so the fighting on the beach wasn't intense by then. He re-enacted the scene of a Japanese soldier who ran across the beach. Tony pointed out several landmarks and hills and Dad recalled them.

It was getting near the time for the ceremony and meeting Governor Gutierrez. We drove to a cinder block civic center/senior center and went inside. Several people were gathered for this ceremony and luncheon. The local U.S. Navy commander of the naval base was there, a reporter from the Pacific Stars and Stripes was there. The vice-mayor, Joaquin Topasna, and several senior citizens who were World War II occupation survivors were also in attendance.

Governor Gutierrez arrived with his entourage. He was a most hospitable, friendly man. He treated us as honored guests. The awards ceremony began. Governor Gutierrez explained to my dad that he was receiving the Ancient Order of the Chamorri Award; the Guamanians were of the Chamorri people group. This is the highest civilian award that a governor could bestow upon a non-Guamanian. He told my father that receiving such an award basically said, "You are now a Guamanian." Dad accepted the award humbly, stated he would only accept the award if he could accept it for all of the U.S. servicemen who fought to liberate Guam, especially those who fell. Dad choked up at this point and then regained his composure. Dad also received a Guamanian flag, which when he came home flew under the American flag on the flagpole in his front yard. He told the governor that Guam is a beautiful island. He said it was even beautiful 51 years ago, but in a different way. He was happy and proud to be part of the effort to liberate Guam. Claps and handshakes and exchange of gifts and photo ops then occurred.

We settled in for a wonderful Guamanian-style luau on the beach of Agat Bay. My dad was a finicky eater and not too interested in Asian seafood. I coached him before to "fake it" and eat what was presented. He did okay. He and the governor sat down together and had a great lunchtime conversation. They conversed with each other like old friends.

Afterwards, we went back into the hall. There the senior citizen Guamanians were busy seriously playing mah jong, an Oriental dominoes game. We watched and when it was time for us to go, they stopped the game, lined up, and one by one received Dad. They would grab my dad's hand with both of their hands and say, "Thank you; you are my lee-borator." One by one they passed by, thanking Dad for what he had done. I don't believe anyone had ever really thanked my dad for his sacrifices. These people wholeheartedly did and they meant it. They were freed from the tyranny of the Japanese by the effort of the Marines, the Army, and the Navy. And my dad was part of that effort 51 years ago.

Dad and I said our goodbyes to the governor and thanked him and Tony and his staff. We got back in the rental car. I started the car and was busy turning on the AC to defog the windows and I was pretty stoked about what had just transpired. I turned to Dad and asked what he wanted to do now, and then I looked at Dad. He was sitting in the passenger seat, his hands were shaking; his voice was quivering. He was absolutely blown away by what had just happened. I think that those senior citizens thanking him was more than he had ever expected. He asked if we could wait a few minutes while he collected his thoughts and composure.

After Dad recovered we went to our final tour of the Orote Peninsula where the Marines final battle on Guam pushed the enemy off the cliffs. We then went back to the airport and boarded our plane for Hawaii and Pearl Harbor. We landed in Hawaii, regained a day, and refreshed ourselves at the Queen Kapiolani Hotel. That night after dinner, Dad and I marched in cadence in front of the Moana Hotel on Kalakaua Avenue where his cousin and he had a picture taken 51 years earlier. The following morning we took the tour of Pearl Harbor. My dad had visited Pearl Harbor three or four times before; this was my first venture.

A movie is shown before you take the tour. It is a very pro-American film and the narration does not paint a pleasant picture of what the Japanese did. I remember that sitting right behind me was a tour group from Japan and I could hear one man interpreting the narration to the tour group. The tour group sat silently as the interpreter told what had happened.

We boarded a tour boat and went out to the USS Arizona. What a solemn occasion that was. But the interesting thing to note was Dad stood there and he said, "This is the first time I've been out here and not cried. I guess I'm getting over this." His acknowledgment made me feel good. I realized that perhaps this last year of discussions and research and reading and talking and walking over the old battlefields was giving my father some needed closure on old wounds.

"When I was a kid, I was exactly like you are. I wanted to be a hero. That's why I joined the Air Force, so I could be somebody. Let me tell you something, Davey. Heroes don't just shoot bad guys. They put supper on the table. They fix bicycles. They do boring things; real things."

Colonel Hal Osborne, talking to his son, David in the movie,
"Cloak & Dagger" (Tom Holland)

CHAPTER 14

Of Heroes and Medals

My father was a highly decorated World War II Marine. He trained for years, traveled over 32,000 miles to fight in two battles, Guam and direct front line on Sugar Loaf. He suffered from dysentery, dengue, jungle rot and fleas, and he sustained wounds on Sugar Loaf and Mezado Ridge. He suffered psychological injury with the loss of his cousin David and the loss of his platoon on Sugar Loaf Hill.

He received a Purple Heart and a Gold Star in lieu of a second Purple Heart. He, along with all the men who fought on Sugar Loaf Hill that night, were to be awarded some decoration according to a conversation he had with some commanding officer the morning he returned from the hill. Lieutenant Pesely did receive a Silver Star and Major Courtney the Medal of Honor. Colonel Woodhouse, who would have made the recommendation, was killed by a sniper before he could fulfill that promise. I always felt that my dad deserved a Bronze or Silver Star. He balked at the idea. He contended that those who died were the real heroes and those that survived should honor that. While I understood that sentiment, I began to investigate in 1996 the possibility of my dad receiving a Bronze or Silver Star. I discussed this with a good friend and patient, (Robert) Bruce Brown, he himself a Vietnam-era veteran Marine sergeant and currently second in command of the Oregon Veterans' Affairs. He was at the time quite busy running around the state giving World War II veterans the medals they had earned, yet through some bureaucratic snafu, never received. It was one of Mr. Brown's most cherished assignments. He told me that the process was tedious and onerous. Old records needed to be found, and most importantly eyewitness accounts were needed to attest to the action. It is one thing that my dad clearly remembered what occurred on Sugar Loaf Hill that evening in May of 1945, but of the 150 Marines on the hill that night, only 10 crawled off alive in the morning. Lieutenant Pesely did not even remember my dad when he called 50 years later. Mr. Pesely had suffered a bit of battle fatigue after that horrendous night on Sugar Loaf.

My only hope was to ask Ed Pesely to testify. I wrote him and asked him whether he could. He wrote me back.

July 1, 1996

Dear Jay:

This is in response to your letter of April 5, 1996, regarding your father and his participation in the Battle of Sugar Loaf Hill. First, I would like to say that your father should be very proud of a son who feels so strongly about his dad and his wartime experience. And I certainly agree with your assessment that everyone who was on Sugar Loaf Hill on the night that Courtney led us forward deserves a medal, even posthumously as Courtney himself received his. I doubt, however, if everyone received one; but I honestly don't know who got medals for that night and who didn't.

You probably know that it is usually left to the individual's own commanding officer — or other qualified witness — to recommend him for a medal. And although as you discovered, there are procedures for remedying serious oversights such as you believe to be your father's situation, it does take one or more eye witnesses to vouch for the heroic actions that merit the medal.

Unfortunately, there was so much confusion on that terrible night on Sugar Loaf Hill, I can only recall that my battalion commander gave me 27 men as replacements for our dead and wounded — and of those 27 men — two were said to be officers. According to your father's account, it would seem that he was one of those officers, and if so, his exploits were probably as he remembers them. But I have no distinct recollection of his activities that night, so I could not now — 50 years later — serve your cause as a credible witness. That is not to say that perhaps some of the other replacements — or other replacement lieutenant who came with him — might now have a better remembrance of your father's deeds that night than I have.

I am truly sorry that I can't be more helpful to you in what seems a just cause, but the facts that I remember are as I stated them, and I'm sure that your father would not want, nor accept, a medal based solely on his son's passionate appeal.

If your father does not get a medal for his heroic actions on that hill, he will be in good company. Many of the original members of the 1st Provisional Marine Brigade (later the 6th Marine Division) spent almost three years overseas and participated in three previous amphibious assaults against heavily defended beaches, and only a few received medals they all deserved.

We have a saying in the 22ⁿᵈ Marines: "Medals don't make you a hero and not all heroes get medals." Only the individual knows what he did and with or without a medal, nobody can take that away from him. Please give my fondest regards to your father and tell him he should be proud to have a son like you.

Semper Fi,

Ed Pesely."

I wrote Mr. Pesely back and said:

"Dear Mr. Pesely:

Thank you very much for your kind and thoughtful letter of July 1, 1996. I really did believe that it was a shot in the dark to get my father awarded a Silver or Bronze Star. However, I thought I would try.

It is quite apparent to me from all my readings and discussions that that night was a terrifically confusing one, and to try to recall anything 50 years later would be something short of miraculous. At any rate, in my mind my father will always be a hero, and like the 22ⁿᵈ Marines said, "Medals don't make you a hero and not all heroes get medals." That puts this totally in perspective for me. Thank you very much for your time and consideration. God bless you.

Semper Fi,

Jay Jamieson, M.D."

I never told my dad I did this. Mom knew and somewhat sternly told me that Dad would not be interested in such a pursuit. With the only witness not remembering anything, I shelved the idea.

But Dad was and always will be a hero to me. I really had to ask myself what I was trying to prove by attempting to have my father recognized with a medal. It was probably more about me than him. I remember recently watching the movie "Flags of Our Fathers," and the final narrative when the Marines are down taking a swim after the battle, the narrator says (John Bradley's son, James) the following:

"I finally came to the conclusion that maybe he was right. Maybe there is no such thing as heroes. Maybe there are just people like my dad. I finally came to understand why the men were so uncomfortable being called heroes. Heroes are something **we** create, something **we** need. It's a way for us to understand what is almost incomprehensible; how people could sacrifice so much for us. But for my dad and these men, the risks they took, the wounds they suffered, they did that for their buddies. They may have fought for their country but they died for their friends. For the men in front, for the men beside them, and if we wish to truly honor these men, we would remember them the way they truly were, the way my dad remembered them." ¹³

That was beautifully put. I couldn't express it any better.

"Hey, maybe the time just wasn't right to hang on. When are you gonna learn
Sometimes things turn instead of turn out?
Hey, when are you gonna stand and stop looking over your shoulder?
Me, with a head full of words and not one useful expression.
Hey............ let go."

from Begin, a song by Nicky Mehta of the Wailin' Jennys

"If the Army and the Navy ever look on Heaven's scenes, they will find the streets are guarded by United States Marines"

last line from the Marine Corps Hymn

"We miss you so much, Rog, especially your wry wit and wonderful sense of humor that sustained you and your family during your final illness."

from the obituary written by Betty, wife of 62 years.

CHAPTER 15

Let Go

The trip was over and, in my opinion, was more successful than I could ever have imagined. We found all the places Dad wanted to re-visit. We met new friends. Dad received thanks and recognition that he would never have sought, but was none-the –less deserved.

When Dad returned home, a prolific letter writing effort ensued. He wrote Ed Pesley and was invited to meet with the 6th Marine Division Officer's Association. They met annually for a guest speaker and luncheon at the M.C.R.D. in San Diego. The meeting date was on or around April 1st each year, commemorating the landing day on Okinawa. He enjoyed belonging to that exclusive group of men. He had a chance to listen and share experiences with the men who had been there. As the years went by, my older brother, David, also a Marine veteran would go with Dad and also had a great time.

One of Dad's friends from his hometown, Gordon Erickson, invited Dad to speak at a local men's club. Dad prepared a speech and gave the talk and answered questions. The speech was an excellent synopsis of the trip, quite honest and candid and showed me that Dad could discuss these issues in public. This was more evidence that Dad had come to terms with his war experience. Dad made his peace with his past, as best he could. He could talk about these events now without getting choked up.

Dad wrote back and forth with his old World War II buddy, Rex Dillow and visited him in Missouri once. They shared and recollected what had occurred since their separation over fifty years earlier. It turned out that on the morning of May 15, 1945 when Dad was called off Sugar Loaf wounded, Rex was leading a platoon within a hundred yards of Dad, running interference so the Marines could get off the hill safely. Neither men knew how close they were to each other that morning in 1945 until they reunited and began comparing notes on their Okinawa experiences fifty years later.

Rex, Dad would find out, fought on in Okinawa and had a near death experience being buried alive when an enemy explosive caved in his fox hole.

Dad also learned that Rex re-enlisted in 1952 and was shipped off to Korea. His first assignment was the Chosin Reservoir: "The Frozen Chosin". And when Rex survived Korea, he remained in the Corps and finished up his career in Vietnam, retiring with the rank of colonel in 1970.

Dad wrote a letter to all of his surviving cousins about his experience on Saipan and sent them all a copy of the governor's proclamation. He received nice letters back.

Dad corresponded with Jack Grant soon after our trip to Saipan and Okinawa. They shared their World War II experiences and what it felt like to lose men. The two connected. The two men experienced a bond that can only occur between warriors. Both men had led Marines into battle. Both men had lost Marines under their charge. Jack's and Dad's relationship intersected through David Dougherty. Both mourned his untimely death. And although it may seem obvious to the outsider that they did nothing wrong, both carried a sense of guilt, sadness and remorse their entire lives. It is a complex set of emotions that those of us who have never been placed in a similar situation cannot fully comprehend. We can imagine what it would feel like, but only the surviving warrior knows. Jack wrote Dad about these feelings and Dad responded, "Jack, I was touched by your letter…., and I am able to relate to your feelings. When you are a squad leader (and I was a sergeant once myself) or a platoon leader, you don't want one of them to get the runs; when it comes to the case of getting killed (many of my young men were killed on Sugar Loaf Hill), it's something you carry with you the rest of your life. And nobody can tell you to drop it. I still feel responsible for my cousin, Dave; he joined the Marines because I did."

Dad was invited to the annual 2nd Squad, 3rd platoon, C-1-25 reunion, to be held at Alexandria in August 1996. My brother Doug and I went with Dad. We had a great time. It was wonderful to meet these men after corresponding with them and learning their history. I had sent them pictures of Yellow II and some sand from the beach. Leo Kelly introduced me to Chesapeake Bay blue crab cakes. Delicious! We all sat around at our first dinner and Lance raised his glass and toasted David Dougherty. "He was a good lad and we miss him." All present raised their glasses to toast and honor him, "To David". That was a poignant moment for the visiting Jamiesons who had been invited into the inner circle of the squad.

The following morning, Lance joined Doug, Dad and me for a walk to the Capitol Mall. We visited the Vietnam and Korean Memorials and talked. Lance wanted to talk to Dad about that day, June 15, 1944 when the squad was hit on the landing attempt. Lance was standing on the amtrac right in front of David Dougherty when the mortar hit. He explained that all on board were rendered unconscious for a period. Lance woke up to find himself drowning in a pool of salt water and blood in the bottom of the amtrac. David was on top of him and Lance struggled to get up to breathe. David was conscious and dazed and seriously wounded, called out for his mother and died quietly. Lance thought we would want to know that, and Dad was grateful to hear the story.

We bonded with the squad and Dad visited the Grant's home later on and revisited the squad at another reunion on the Jersey shore at Charlie Wolf's place. Mom went with him that time.

Jack Grant's squad still gets together. As he puts it, "those still standing remain just as close and united as we were 70 years ago. Proof of this is our record of 15 annual reunions, which to our knowledge is unheard of in WWII Marine reunions."

As for me, the trip was gratifying on many levels. For one, it was the only time in my entire life that I had the undivided attention of my father for 2 weeks. Growing up in a medium sized family, we did most things as a group: family vacations (we even all slept together in hotels on 2 double beds) dinners and movies, baseball and scouts. Since I had left for college in 1971 I have never lived closer to home than 600 miles. So the "Fourteen Days with Rog", as my brother Douglas came to call our trip, was a priceless gift to me. We had great talks and shared some wonderful times together.

I got to meet a whole group of heroes from the Greatest Generation. They all had a story or two to tell and if you asked, they would talk. One particular meeting was with Joseph Sheridan from Massachusetts. He was the current president of the 1st Marine Division Association. I met him on a bus ride in Okinawa. There happened to be only four of us on the bus heading off to some evening banquet. I turned to Mr. Sheridan, seeing that he had served in the 1st Marine Division, who had an artificial arm, and asked him if he had fought at Guadacanal in 1942. "Yeah, what's it to ya?" was his rather brisk retort. Dad looked on as I politely explained that I had read several books and articles and watched some video documentaries about the battle and I had some questions about the battle. I had never met a veteran of that battle before. I introduced him to my dad, a fellow Marine and he seemed to ease up a bit.

I asked him what he felt like when the Marines were essentially abandoned by the Navy on the island and left to fend for themselves. No one thought the Marines would survive and no re-supply system was set up. They were left to their own devices. Was he scared or angry? "What were we supposed to do? We were kids. I was eighteen years old; I had never been out of Massachusetts before. This was the biggest adventure of our lives. There was no time for pity or worry. At night if we would hear a noise, we would shoot first and ask questions later. One night we hit something out there moving. The following morning we discovered we hit a water buffalo. We cleaned it and cut it up and shared it with all the men."

Against all odds, the 1st Marine Division defeated the Japanese and claimed the island. New Zealand and Australia were saved from a Japanese invasion because of these men's heroics. I asked him if he had fought on Okinawa. He said he had not. He lost his arm fighting on Bougainville. He was here at the official capacity of president of the 1st Marine Division Association. He went on to express his frustration with the VA health care system as it related to the care of his arm. That didn't surprise me, as I had worked several times in V.A. hospitals.

It was an honor to learn first hand what Sgt. Grant's Squad endured in battle and the mental anguish they endured since and to be able to shake the survivor's hands and thank them. They are true heroes.

And when I came home, I came to realize that many of my Medicare aged patients were World War II veterans and I found out that , one by one, each had a unique story to tell, if I took the time to ask. It became a privilege and honor to be their doctor and learn from them. To all our veterans of all the wars, I thank you for your service and sacrifice.

As Tom Brokaw stated in his book, Greatest Generation,: "When the war was over, the men and women who had been involved, in uniform and civilian capacities, joined in a joyous and short-lived celebration, then immediately began the task of building their lives and the world they wanted." Dad came home, got married, found work and played semi-pro baseball with his father's team, the Chevrolet Red Sox. The birth of Lynn and then David and a near death encounter with bulbar polio would force Dad to hang up his cleats for the last time. Doug and I would show up in the early fifties. Dad would go on to coach his boys in baseball and assist in Boys Scouts.

Fulfilling a dream that was planted when he visited California in the forties during his Marine training at Camps Pendleton and Elliot, Dad moved us in 1965 to California from New Jersey when a job opportunity came up with ITT at Vandenberg Air Force Base in Lompoc. Dad finished his career in aerospace defense management. He believed a strong military would be a deterrent and would keep his children from having to go to war as he and his cousin did.

In August 2006, Dad called me to say he had been diagnosed with prostate cancer and within a week a bone scan revealed the disease had advanced to his bones. This was surprising to all, as Dad had been a stickler his whole life for annual exams and PSA checks. But, unfortunately, this cancer slipped under the radar.

He took the treatments offered him over the next several months, but by February 2007, it was becoming apparent to me that he was losing his battle. Dad kept his eternal optimism up until the end.

Dad made his peace with God before he died. He knew he was going to heaven. Roger died peacefully at his home on June 3, 2007 with his loving wife, Betty, and daughter Lynn at his side.

Although I had talked with him by phone several times before he died, I last was with him on April 22, 2007. I had visited for 4 days and I had to leave for the airport to catch a flight home. Dad was lying in bed, thin and pale, covered up under a quilt. There he was; a shell of a man. I had to say goodbye and I knew I would not be seeing him again this side of heaven. Although we didn't speak it, he knew it too. I grabbed his hand and told him I was proud of him and that he was so brave. I told him I was praying for him every day. He said 'I know." Tears welled up. "I love you, Dad." I said. "I love you, too," he replied. I kissed him on his forehead and left. I lost it outside his bedroom.

Dad, with the help of Mom, raised his children to be honest, hard working self-reliant individuals. As my sister Lynn so concisely expressed in her eulogy to Dad, "He exposed us to a scrupulously crafted honesty, and in doing so, expected us to be truthful, face the consequences of our actions, and set it right if we were wrong." We who knew him, and were so privileged to have been called his family and were blessed to have been his, now had to let him go. I have heard it said that the type of relationship we had with our earthly father influences how we perceive and relate to our Heavenly Father. Fortunately for me and thanks to the example of the life of my dad, I understand about God's love, discipline, mercy and grace. Roger Jamieson was human and far from perfect, but I consider myself blessed to be called his son. Thank you, Dad. And while we, his children and grandchildren will try to live up to his example, it will prove to be too lofty a goal. Daniel Fogleberg's song, <u>Leader of the Band,</u> sums it all up this way: "My life has been a poor attempt to imitate the man; I'm just a living legacy to the leader of the band."

Semper fi, Dad. You done good, Rog. We love you and we miss you and we'll meet again some sunny day.........

The Chronology of the Career of Captain Roger Jamieson, USMCR

Active Service

7 April 1942 - Enlist in USMCR at Philadelphia Navy Yard

10 April 1942 – Appointed a PFC, USMCR (service number 397470) at Philadelphia Navy Yard

11 August 1942 – Began active duty in 10th. Candidates' Class, Quantico

October 1942 – Washed out of OCS, opted to stay in USMC, transferred to New River, assigned to Headquarters and Service Company, First Separate Battalion, FMF, MB

24 October 1942 – Appointed a Corporal (temporary)

January or February 1943 – Appointed a Sergeant

Late winter or early spring 1943 – First Separate Battalion transferred to Camp Pendleton and Became part of newly formed 4th Marine Division

May 1943 – Sent to Camp Elliot for officer screening

June 1943 – Transferred to 31st. Candidates' Class, Quantico

10 August 1943 – Honorably discharged as Sergeant to accept appointment as Second Lieutenant

11 August 1943 – Appointed a Second Lieutenant (temporary) (service number 028435)

20 October 1943 – Completed 34th. Reserve Officers' Class

6 November 1943 – Reported to Headquarters, Camp Lejeune, New River and further reported to 37th. Replacement Battalion, Co. B

22 November 1943 to 14 January 1944 – 6th. Rifle Platoon Class, Training Center, Camp Lejeune

20 January 1944 – Ordered to permanent duty beyond the seas

28 March 1944 – Detached from Headquarters, Transient Center, V Amphibious Corps, c/o Fleet Post Office, San Francisco and reported to 1st. Provisional Marine Brigade

17 April 1944 (on or about) – Boarded ship for Guadalcanal (BEVY)

21 July 1944 – W-Day, Guam

7 September 1944 – 1st. Provisional Marine Brigade re-designated the 6th. Marine Division

31 January 1945 – Promoted to First Lieutenant (temporary)

1 April 1945 – D-Day, Okinawa

13 May 1945 (on or about) – Transferred from Signal Co., Headquarters Battalion, 6th. Marine Division to F Co., 2d. Bn., 22d Regt., 6th. Marine Division

14 May 1945 (on or about) – Wounded on Sugar Loaf Hill

16 May 1945 (on or about) – Transferred by air to Guam hospital

20 May 1945 (on or about) – Released from hospital and transferred to Casual Battalion, Transient Center, Marianas

31 May 1945 (on or about) – Determined to be "Class A"; opted to return to Okinawa instead of transferring to Rear Echelon, 6th. Marine Division, Guam

10 June 1945 – Left on S.S. Fairland

11 June 1945 – Arrived Saipan

12 June 1945 – Departed Saipan

16 June 1945 - Arrived at Okinawa

17 June 1945 – Opted to stay with F-2-22 instead of returning to Head-quarters Bn., 6th. Marine Division; wounded by sniper fire en route to front

18 June 1945 – transported to USS Rescue via LST (H) 730 (or 930)

19 June 1945 – Departed Okinawa

23 June 1945 – Admitted to U.S. Naval Base Hospital #18, Guam, Marianas Islands

4 July 1945 – Discharged to duty at Casual Battalion, Transient Center, Forward Echelon, FMF, Pacific, c/o FPO, San Francisco

5 July 1945 – Reported to Rear Echelon, 22nd. Marines, 6th. Marine Division

9 July 1945 – Reported to Casual Battalion, Transient Center, Marianas Area

16 July 1945 – Reported on board USS Long Island (CVE-1) for transportation to Pearl Harbor (FRAY), reporting on arrival to CG, FMF, Pacific for further transportation to the United States where I would proceed to Camp Pendleton

17 July 1945 – Departed Guam

27 July 1945 – Arrived at Pearl Harbor

29 July 1945 – Departed Pearl Harbor

4 August 1945 – Reported to Headquarters, Department of the Pacific, Marine Corps, 100 arrison Street, San Francisco; given delay until 2400 17 Sept. '45; several Days after reporting taken to U.S. Naval Hospital, Brooklyn: hepatitis

16 November 1945 – Discharged from hospital, returned to MB, NAD, Lake Denmark, Dover

22 May 1946 – Relieved from active duty

Reserve Service

14 March 1949 – promotion to First Lieutenant made permanent via Third Marine Corps Reserve District, N.Y., N.Y.

26 March 1951 – Promoted to Captain from 7 January '49 via Third Marine Corps Reserve District

12 August 1957 – Accepted for membership in Volunteer Training Unit (VTU) G 1-34, USMCR, First Marine Corps Reserve and Recruitment District, Garden City, Long Island, N.Y.

7 July 1961 – Cancellation of VTU membership as of 1 July '61

1 December 1961 – Transferred to Retired Reserve after honorable service

ADDENDUM

ROGER JAMIESON'S MEMORIAL SERVICE WAS HELD ON
JUNE 15, 2007
Santa Ynez Valley Presbyterian Church
Eulogy by Douglas Jamieson:

At Roger's funeral service the speakers were: son, Doug Jamieson; here is what he had to say:

"And now for something completely different!" For those of you who know "Monty Python," you'll recognize those words. My dad loved Monty Python. He appreciated all kinds of comedians. From Jackie Gleason to Steve Martin. From Johnny Carson to Bill Murray. His top 10 movie list is basically a compilation of Mel Brooks films, for to him, Mel Brooks was a comic genius. Dad once said that the campfire scene in "Blazing Saddles" was by itself worthy of an Oscar nomination.

My Dad had great nicknames for people and things.

Ruth Erickson – Nancy nicely

SY Valley News – Valley Astonisher

Jay's boys – The piranha brothers

Mom – Bet, Kid, or Nurse Jane Fuzzy Wuzzy

We are blessed and grateful that Dad was cared for by Betty up to his last breath. Mom, your care, love and compassion for Dad the last nine months was, well, there are no words to describe it. We should all be so lucky when our days come to an end. We love you and thank you. And we know how you'll miss your husband, your best friend, your companion.

For my Dad, baseball played a central role. When Mom and Dad went to Arizona for the Giant's spring training one year, he was interviewed in the stands by the local Scottsdale newspaper. He was quoted as saying his earliest childhood memory was when he was 5 years old at Yankee Stadium. His Uncle Chuck was in town playing against the Yankees. Charlie Jamieson played 16 years for the Cleveland Indians. Uncle Chuck came over and picked Dad out of the stands and carried him across the diamond to meet one of the Yankee players. That player was Babe Ruth.

So baseball became a passion for Dad. He didn't get to play much on his high school team or during his first 2 years at Muhlenberg College. But when he was finally given the chance to start at second base his junior year, he never looked back. He got to play after the war in Paterson with a couple of semi-pro teams into his 30's.

While in the Marine Corps, he was asked to play 2nd base for the Marine Corps baseball team. This would allow him to avoid any fighting and live out his days in the Corps traveling from here to there, playing baseball against other service teams and semi-pro teams. My Dad said no, that wasn't the reason he joined the Marine Corps.

Dad played catch with Dave, Jay and me. He taught us how to play baseball, but he also taught us about the game of baseball which he loved so passionately. Baseball offered up some simple life lessons as well: Sometimes you don't get the call you deserve, but the game goes on.

Suit up and show up...I cannot remember my Dad ever being home sick from work.

I think my dad liked the rules of baseball. They were straightforward and clear-cut. And that was how Dad lived his life.

Dad coached Little League teams both in New Jersey and here in the valley. In New Jersey, there's a story about a playoff game he coached where one of his players hit a long fly ball out of the park that was ruled foul by the umpire. My Dad called time out, and with his hands tucked into his back pockets, approached the plate ump, just a 16-year-old kid. Dad simply held up one hand and said, I just wanted to ask him if he understood the rule that it didn't matter if the ball curved "foul" after it left the park, that as long as it was fair when it went over the fence, it should be a home run. The kid said that indeed he knew that rule.

Dad went up to his batter and said, "Do it again." And he did. In fact, as legend has it, it was an exact replay of the previous ball hit. The ump ruled it a home run.

When he got to California and the SY Valley, Dad again volunteered to coach Little League. The league asked him to take a couple of boys that, well, no one seemed to be able to control or manage. You see, Tom and Sam Johnson had lost their Dad in a car accident a few years earlier and it was a little rough at the Johnson house. My Dad said no problem.

And as it turned out, it was no problem. It was actually the beginning of a lifelong friendship with the Johnson family. In fact, Dad requested that Marge sing today—we were a little concerned about giving a microphone to Marge with a captive audience—but that's OK—We love you, Marge, and you were OK in Rog's book.

To be "OK" in Rog's book was the highest form of compliment from my Dad. He had a special way with words. An afternoon of swimming and eating at Rob & Bet's house on 3084 Country Rd. was called having a "swim out." We all miss those. When he asked for the salt and pepper at the dinner table, it was "Pass the peppy poo please."

In 1987 and 1989, Connie, Betty, Rog and I got to share the excitement of Giants playoff baseball in San Francisco. After one particularly great game, the four of us found ourselves sharing a single hotel room with two beds. As we talked into the night about the game, Dad popped out of bed to demonstrate for us how Robbie Thompson gloved a grounder and threw someone out at first. There he was, crouched between the 2 beds in his boxers and a T-shirt when, from the far side of the bed, we heard Betty's voice, "Rog, go to sleep." He giggled and jumped back into bed.

In 2002, I got to take my Dad to a World Series game. The Giants didn't win that day, but that didn't matter. It was a great day. In fact, I think being at the ballpark was for my Dad like a little bit of heaven on earth. And sometimes it didn't matter if the Giants won or lost, unless they were playing the Dodgers.

When spring training came around this year, I think we all realized this would probably be Dad's last season. And in the game of life, when Rog got to the ninth inning and we realized there would probably be no last-minute heroics or miracle home runs, my Dad stoically and humbly accepted his fate. With that in mind, I gain comfort knowing the following:

If there is such a thing as God's "Universal All-Star Team," there surely is a spot open for a sure-handed, slap-hitting, speedy 2nd baseman, a Marine, a great father and husband, a man who always seemed to say, and more importantly, to do the Right Thing.

I LOVE YOU AND I MISS YOU, DAD!!!

Eulogy by Jay Jamieson:

It is good to be home again with family and friends here in this sanctuary. I can recall many good memories here. Today, in many ways, is a sad day. We have to say goodbye for now to a dear one, our family's patriarch: husband, father, uncle, great uncle, grandfather, great-grandfather and friend.

But today is a joyful day as we reflect on our Dad as a wonderful man who lived a full life. We thank God for giving him to us. We are blessed to say he loved us.

Dad displayed many virtues that he lived out quietly every day, and I could speak about all of them: Self-discipline, compassion, responsibility, friendship, loyalty, work ethic, honesty, perseverance, and always faithful Semper Fidelis.

All of this with a humility and an optimism and a sense of humor. He modeled these virtues not by preaching but by living them out daily.

Dad's legacy lives on in his children and grandchildren. We are, after all, "Chips off the Old Block."

Lynn: Last Word Louise – driven work ethic, love of writing and fiercely loyal to her family. If one of our family were under attack, Lynn would always be there to our aid.

Dave: Big Red – Bats L and throws R, by far the best baseball player of the three brothers, a Marine and politically conservative.

Doug: Dugo – the consummate SF Giants fan, scrappy business negotiator, prolific reader. And he, like me, inherited Dad's ineptitude with tools and home repairs.

Me: Last Word Louie – Difficult to judge myself: a bureaucratic Administrator, frugal and hey, somebody had to inherit Dad's good looks and wit.

But the one virtue I would like to focus on was Dad's courage. I never met a braver man. He never backed down when a wrong needed to be confronted by right. He had the gift of discernment in choosing the battle and defining the battle lines.

If we, his children, found ourselves in a scrape, he would want the facts straight from us. We would receive a reckoning talk and then he would be our greatest advocate when we had to face the music, making sure the punishment met the crime.

He wasn't afraid of anything or anybody. He was the rock of our family: feet firmly planted on the ground. When any of us were from time to time in sinking sand, there was Dad to help us sort out the pieces, distill the issues, and help set us straight again. Sometimes it came as a keen insight or a word of encouragement. Sometimes all we needed was a swift boot in the rear. But he was our constant encourager and protector.

I asked him once where that bravery came from. He told me, referring back to his WWII experiences as Marine officer on Guam and Okinawa, "Jay, they already tried to kill me twice, what else can they do to me?"

And that was true. What else could life throw at him? The defining period in our Dad's life was his WWII Marine Corps training and service in the Pacific. The Corps took his raw talents and refined them and that defined who Dad would be. The lessons learned would carry him for the next 62-plus years.

Dad faced several battles in his life including WWII, his bout with polio, raising teens in the 60s and 70s, the loss of a grandchild, Roger Douglas, and finally his recent bout with cancer. Like a true Marine officer, he faced these challenges without complaint; he stared the enemy straight in its face like he did in battle on Sugar Loaf Hill on May 15, 1945, and marched forward bravely. He never shirked his duty.

Dad suffered physical and emotional wounds from his WWII experiences. He lost several men under his command on Sugar Loaf Hill. His beloved cousin, David Leslie Dougherty, was killed in action on this very day, June 15, 1944, attempting to land on Saipan with the 4th Marine Division. Dad didn't dwell on these matters or complain. He did what the majority of the Greatest Generation did. He came home from the war, got married, went to work, raised a family and served the community.

In 1995, Dad revisited some old WWII battle sights and got some closure on the emotional battle wounds. On Guam, the governor held a luau in Dad's honor and bestowed upon him Guamanian citizenship. On Saipan, he visited the landing beach where his cousin died and he laid a wreath. The Governor declared the day "David Leslie Dougherty Day." And Dad re-climbed Sugar Loaf Hill; this time up a flight of stairs and a Marine Corps Band was playing on top. He stood on the hill and shook hands with his former foe and now new friend, Lt. Shizuo Uzumi, as they together held a Rising Sun Flag.

And with his final battle with cancer, Dad made his peace with God. He knew he was going to heaven. I did write him a letter in March and among other things, I told him to look for two handsome young men who have been patiently waiting for him at the Gates: his cousin David and his grandson, Roger. What a joyous homecoming that must have been. In summary, Dad was our hero. A hero for what he did in battle and more so for what he did raising us. We will try to live up to his example, but that is a lofty goal. Like the last line in Daniel Fogelberg's song, "Leader of the Band," it says, "My life has been a poor attempt to imitate the man; I'm just a living legacy to the leader of the band."

Goodbye for now, Pop. Happy Father's Day. Happy Birthday. We love you. We will miss you every day. And now we let you go into God's most merciful hands until we see you again.

Eulogy by Lynn Jamieson:

Dad died last week after a heroic battle with an unkind disease, and he has left a legacy for his wife, children, grandchildren, great-grandchildren, extended family, friends, and acquaintances impossible to duplicate but a challenge to emulate. During his illness, I found myself telling concerned colleagues and friends that he could have died in World War II or during his bout with polio, but from the time he was 31 to 85 he had very little in the way of illness, and for that we can be thankful. He lived a full and loving life, with a sense of humor that no one can describe.

There are so many things I could tell you about the life that Dad led, particularly his early years in New Jersey, where we were raised – 45 minutes from New York – such a drastic difference from the pastoral setting where we moved in 1965. Suffice it to say that Dad came from humble beginnings with simple pleasures including a value of education, a love of the national pastime, and the value of family. He worked his way through college and then became a hero in World War II, raised this family in unison with our Mom, and the rest is a legacy that will be carried out again and again with our large and growing family. I am, along with my brother David, more of the New Jersey connection to Dad, since David was a junior in high school when Dad made his drive across the country to California in my freshman year of college, and Jay and Doug were in elementary school. We saw Dad in several jobs including Chevy salesman, insurance, and contract administration.

I will focus on his honesty and integrity, his love of education, and his love for our family. Our Dad never took shortcuts where ethics were concerned. He exposed us to a scrupulously crafted honesty, and in doing so, expected us to be truthful, face the consequences of our actions, and set it right if we were wrong. By the same token, there was no one more ferocious when we were wronged – when we were growing up Dad would get to the bottom of a problem by talking to anyone who caused us a problem, checking out details, visiting teachers, principals, school officials, neighbors, friends, strangers. If we got in trouble, he saw to it that we dealt with the consequences.

In matters of money, he was frugal and created interesting ways for us to handle our allowances, jobs, and money matters. All of us were expected to save. We started with our first jobs. Five-sixths of everything I ever earned starting with babysitting went into the bank; this was no insignificant amount when it turned out that I could cover half of my college education in a private school. He also gave each grandchild a yearly allowance that consisted of a graduated amount per week ranging from 50 cents to

$3.00 for school-age children given annually with a great and solemn ceremony. His requirement was that the children needed to stay in school, and he needed to be solvent. This was significant considering 11 grandchildren were the recipients of his generosity.

Dad placed the highest value on education. He himself was a learned man, an avid reader, an English major who corrected our English at every misstep – just a month ago, he corrected two grammar errors I made. I found it fascinating that Dad appreciated the first sentence in major novels he read – and would quote them.

My favorite was "Scarlett O'Hara was not beautiful, but men seldom realized it when caught by her charms as the Tarleton twins were." In fact, we each have a part of his extensive book collection, James Michener, Larry McMurtry, Ian Fleming, etc.

To educate us further, Dad would also initiate funny projects that sometimes wouldn't fly – my favorite was in New Jersey on a Sunday afternoon when Dad introduced a new project for us to learn 10 spelling words per week – I even remember the first word – accolade. I think our whining and squirming only caused this to last one week. Another project was for us to be in charge of one aspect each of a trip to Washington DC when I was in high school. We each had a job and it turned out to be the best trip we took at that time – 6 of us belted into a 1960's Chevy Corvair traveling endless hours to our destination. Dad always started his project by saying – "We're going to have fun!"

In matters of love, Dad was the archetype of the father who came home every night, was faithful to our Mom, and involved in his family. When he walked in the door, we jumped on him and he asked for a few minutes – but we always knew he would be there and never wondered where he was. He was a dedicated family man and loved Mom with all his heart. Theirs has been an amazing marriage of love, partnership, friendship, trust, humor, common activities, and family projects. Sometimes they played music and danced in the kitchen; other times they went out to shows and spent time with friends. Many times, there were family and friend gatherings at our house in NJ – barbecues and dinners – that graduated to pool gatherings and barbecues in Santa Ynez. This tradition continues with Dave and Joannie. We all have valued our visits to Mom and Dad in CA – they always had fun and time for all of us.

In many ways, theirs is a fantastic love story, starting as friendship in high school where both were at the top of their class (1 and 2, not sure which was which), and then a whirlwind courtship before Dad shipped out to the Pacific – an elopement on his return, and 61+ years of marriage, give and take, a large family, satisfactory careers, and the best accomplishment of moving to Santa Ynez and living in California.

Dad also had great love for his children, grandchildren, and great-grandchildren – for our sons, he was a pal, a kind and funny man who could joke and make funny comments about the most mundane things – when Ben wanted a cheese sandwich and a chocolate milk for lunch, it was, "A cheese sandwich and a chocolate milk!" With Byron and school, there have been a dozen times when Dad and Mom shared a movie and meal in Santa Barbara with him and Dad liked talking about the movie they viewed and catching up with him in school. He always has seen the best in all of us and we have felt wonderful about it.

As for me, Dad and I were bonded together very early and unusually when we both contracted poliomyelitis in the early 50's – mine was a mild form and Dad's was bulbar, affecting his lungs. Both of us were in the hospital together for three to four weeks and then undertook 5 years of physical therapy. Dad referred to us as polio pals.

Over the years, we would have long middle-of-the-night conversations about everything under the sun. Other times, we could just sit in a room and not talk but totally understand each other. I found that it was hard to not be with Dad during the whole of his illness because of that early bond – it was absolutely essential that I could take part of the journey with him, but I knew that this time I could not be in it for the long haul.

Dad, we will all miss you, and I will miss you greatly, but you are always in our hearts and minds for the way you cared and made each of us feel special and good. You can rest assured that your love and concern for each of us has provided a firm foundation for us to live the best of lives, and we will always define our behavior by the way you and Mom have raised us and cared for our children and others. Goodbye, Polio Pal.

Eulogy by Grandson, James Jamieson:

Walter Roger Jamieson
"Gramp"
Remembrances of our grandfather

There are many things that I can stand before you and say about our grandfather. Here are a few: Whether it was that little sign on the bunkhouse door, "We do not swim in your toilet, so please don't pee in our pool," to his great photogenic smile with the classic line "I AM SMILING!," to educating all of the grandkids about "classic" American movies such as Young Frankenstein and Blazing Saddles, he always had a great sense of humor that has shown through to all his children and grandchildren alike.

One thing that I can really remember about Gramp was he was always supportive of all of us. He would show up at our baseball, football, hockey, basketball, and soccer games, our wrestling matches and dance and music recitals. Keep in mind, sometimes traveling hours to do so, even going out of state to Oregon and Indiana.

Gramp had a whole allowance system set up for all of the grandkids. We would start at a quarter a week and progress up to a few dollars a week by the time we were in high school. I once asked him why he did this. His response, "Because you are my grandchild." That was enough to shut me up about why he gave us money every week. I think the reality of his system really caught up with him when ALL the Oregon kids were all on the allowance at the same time. Having to lug that box of coins all the way to Oregon just one time was enough for him to change the system to a "one lump sum" annually. I won't forget that even after high school, even though I was too old to get an allowance from him, there was still the elbow nudge and a $20 bill slipped to me; "Here's a little hamburger money."

Gramp and my dad started a little tradition that every Friday they would meet at the Red Barn for lunch. I would join them as often as my schedule would allow. He always had a bowl of clam chowder. "Hold the bacon! And could you warm up a little bread and bring some butter?" There were lots of great conversations over the clam chowder. Afterwards he would have a slice of warm berry pie with chocolate ice cream. When it came time to pay, dad and Gramp would rotate every week. For some reason I would show up when my dad had to pay. He swore that Gramp and I had some sort of "arrangement" for that to happen. It became quite the joke around the lunch table. The last time the three of us went to lunch I decided to throw a wrench into the gear box and pay for THEM. Boy, I thought they were going to fall over in their chairs.

The last story that I have is one that all 11 grandkids can relate to: Gramp had a pool at the house on Country Road. He was meticulous about maintaining it for all of us to use. The one major flaw with the pool was just outside the chain-link fence was a walkway with Spanish Pebbles. And of course no one EVER threw those Spanish Pebbles into the pool! But, they always made it to the bottom somehow. Man, that made Gramp HOT! He would spend hours trying to figure out who had thrown the pebbles.

I have some of those pebbles right now that I would like to give to my cousins and my sister, Sara. I would like to introduce all of you to Gramp's grandchildren and great-grandchildren.

(Ask cousins to come up and hand out pebbles).

Roger Jamieson was the best grandfather that all of us could have had. We will miss him dearly. We love you Gramp.

Oh, and Gramp, let's get together for lunch sometime. Have your people call my people.

Bibliography

Brokaw, Tom. The Greatest Generation. New York: Random House, 1998

Brokaw, Tom. An Album of Memories. New York: Random House, 2001

Fiefer, George. Tennozan, The Battle for Okinawa and the Atomic Bomb. New York: Ticknor and Fields, 1992

Jamieson, W.R. and Wolter, S.A. The Baseball Career of Charlie Jamieson, 1999

Scatzkin, Mike. The Ballplayers. New York: William Morrow and Company, 1990

Schneider, Russell, The Cleveland Indians Encyclopedia, 3rd Edition. Champaign, Illinois: Sports Publishing, L.L.C., 2004

Endnotes

[1] Jessie Jamieson King, personal Jamieson Family History

[2] Schneider, page 571

[3] Shatzkin

[4] Schneider, page 198

[5] Jamieson and Wolter, appendix

[6] New York Times, " The Death of Ray Chapman, August 18, 1920

[7] Feifer, page 314

[8] Ibid, page 133

[9] Ibid, page 242

[10] Donovan Brooks, Pacific Stars and Stripes, Friday June 30, 1995, page 6

[11] Ken Burns and Lynn Novick, The War, PBS film Documentary 2007

[12] Donovan Brooks, Pacific Stars and Stripes, unedited interview, June 26, 1995

[13] Flags of Our Fathers, a film by Clint Eastwood, final scene